Cricket

Celebrating The Modern Game Around The World

Cricket

Celebrating The Modern Game Around The World

Philip Brown & Lawrence Booth

Foreword by
Ian Botham

MITCHELL BEAZLEY

Philip Brown

Thanks to all the people who contributed to this book: Vivien Antwi, David Ashdown, Jack Atley, Danny Baker, Mark Baker, Lee Bailey, Scott Barbour, Lawrence Booth, Ian Botham, Don Brown, Margaret Brown, Graham Chadwick, Frank Coppi, Brian Corcoran, David Davies, Nigel Davies, Anthony Devlin, Matt Eades, Patrick Eagar, Charlotte Elder, Dan Evans, Clare Fathers, Stephen Fay, Stu Forster, Claire Gatcum, Johnny Grave, Edd Griffin, Lucinda Harding-Brown, Giulia Hetherington, Tom Jenkins, Peter Kay, Peter Kemp, Kim Lee, Mark Leech, David Luxton, Lesley MacDonald, James McCallum, Clive Mason, Diana Morris, Graham Morris, Adrian Murrell, Rebecca Naden, Madeleine Penny, Keith Perry, Robert Philip, Derek Pringle, Ben Radford, Dick Rayment, Nigel Seymour, Tom Shaw, Clare Skinner, Martin Smith, John Stern, Peter Taylor, Michael Thomas, Imogen Turner, Joanne Turner, Chris Turvey, Phil Walter, Kerry Wedd, and Ben Williams and of course to all the photographers around the world who have taken great cricket pictures over the past twenty-five years.

A huge thank you to designer Doug Cheeseman for all his efforts above and beyond the call of duty.

Special thanks again to Fiona, Emily and Rory Brown for all their love, help and support.

Lawrence Booth

To Mum, Dad, Alex and Francis.

With thanks to Rob Smyth, for his patience, insight and eye for detail.

Cricket: Celebrating The Modern Game Around The World
Philip Brown and Lawrence Booth

Design by Doug Cheeseman

First published in Great Britain in 2005
by Mitchell Beazley, an imprint of Octopus Publishing Group Ltd
2–4 Heron Quays, London E14 4JP

Copyright © Octopus Publishing Group Ltd 2005

ISBN 1 845 33153 2

A CIP record for this book is available from the British Library

Set in Bradlo Slab and Scala

Colour reproduction by Bright Arts, Hong Kong

Printed and bound in Italy by L.E.G.O. S.p.A.

Commissioning Editor Vivien Antwi
Senior Editor Peter Taylor
Executive Art Editor Yasia Williams-Leedham
Copy-editor Rob Smyth
Proofreader Andy Hilliard
Indexer Sue Farr

PREVIOUS PAGE Robert Key assumes an unorthodox position as West Indies opener Chris Gayle hits out during the third Test at Old Trafford.
August 2004

RIGHT James Anderson's attempts to bowl out the University of West Indies XI are lost in the bigger picture.
March 2004

Contents

Foreword

by Ian Botham

The last 25 years have been an exciting time for international cricket. We have seen two all-time great teams in the 1980s West Indians and the current Australians, some fantastic players and we now have Twenty20 to help take the game forward.

In many ways, if you want to be an international cricketer, now is the time to do it. You're on the merry-go-round virtually the whole year, and I for one would have loved that challenge. Perhaps the players don't have as much fun as we did back in the 1980s, but the lads are getting the rewards now, and if you're a good player in a good side, you can make a healthy living.

It's not been so bad for the fans either, especially when it comes to some of the batsmen who have been around. Viv Richards is the best player I have seen by some distance, and I find it very hard to believe he is not the best player of all time. These days, there are the two little geniuses Brian Lara and Sachin Tendulkar, plus the solid technicians Rahul Dravid and Jacques Kallis. And strokemakers like Matthew Hayden, Ricky Ponting and Adam Gilchrist. Even a newcomer like Andrew Strauss has made a terrific impact.

The match I really would have liked to see was Clive Lloyd's West Indians against Steve Waugh's Australians. If both sides were fully fit, I'd probably just have West Indies edging it. Their battery of fast bowlers made them an amazing side. They were the best I ever played against.

But the Aussies have rewritten the way the game is played. Who ever heard of scoring at four an over in Test cricket? In the old days you were doing well to score at more than two. You'd pay to watch this Australian side day in, day out. They've set new benchmarks, and it will be fascinating to see whether any of the other

seven Test nations – I don't count Zimbabwe or Bangladesh – can get near to them in the next few years.

The arrival of Twenty20 is another reason to be optimistic. It's been an injection of pace and excitment in the middle of the English season, and it has caught on in other countries too. I can see the case for starting a Twenty20 World Cup – you could do it in a few days and you'd get huge audiences.

I also hope it will lead to a revamp of the 50-over game, which has become too stereotyped. One innovation I'd like to see is to have two fielders outside the circle for the first 20 overs, but then allow only one more to leave the circle every 10 overs. The players would be encouraged to carry on going for their shots, and you might get the scores you should be making on some of the excellent wickets which are around today.

The rise of sponsorship has changed the face of the game as we know it, and for English cricket the involvement of NatWest over the last 25 years has been particularly crucial. It is incredibly important to have a big-name brand like them providing valuable financial support to all levels of the game, and I know that everyone who works in English cricket has been thoroughly impressed by their commitment.

We should be in for a cracking summer. I hope this book reminds you that we've been lucky enough to have had a few over the last couple of decades too.

Introduction

To the traditionalist, cricket's Golden Age ended when World War One began. To the realist, it is right here, right now. It is hard to believe that the greatest players of the last 25 years would not have thrived alongside the likes of WG Grace and Ranjitsinhji, or that the thrills we are currently experiencing have ever been surpassed on a regular basis in the game's rich history. Cricket fans who have grown up in this colourfully chaotic modern era have been well and truly spoiled.

Yet cricket – or so the stereotype goes – has always had peculiar relationships with past, present and future. The past is a happy time, full of sunlit fields and small boys collecting cigarette cards of their Brylcreemed heroes. The present is forever on the cusp of a crisis. As for the future, well, that went to the dogs a long time ago. The reality, however, has always been a little different.

In 1963, as part of its centenary celebrations, sport's most famous annual *Wisden Cricketers' Almanack* invited its readers to come up with suggestions to improve the English county game. The following year the book printed its findings, and outlined two of the most common responses. "Sunday cricket – after church – plus two divisions with promotion and relegation," and "Permission for overseas stars to play immediately." Overseas players were formally introduced not long after, but the concept of two divisions had to wait until the new millennium. The past was in fact one step ahead of the future, although the concept of Sunday worship might have been taking things a little far.

While most aspects of the game have improved over the last 25 years, new pressures have inevitably accompanied the development. In 1980 you would have been hard pressed to find a batsman reverse-sweeping a doosra, only to be run out by a piece of athleticism at backward point and a referral to the third umpire. But you would have been equally unlikely to find codes of conduct, match referees, and fast bowlers breaking down with stress fractures after playing five Tests back to back, as South Africa and England did last winter. What we can say with some certainty is that, 128 years after the first Test, between Australia and England at the Melbourne Cricket Ground, the international game continues to delight a lot more often than it depresses. And it certainly continues to raise eyebrows.

To this writer, nothing was more surprising than the belated surge of the England team; anyone who followed their halting progress across the past three decades will share the sensation. There were some stirring Ashes triumphs in the 1980s, and one or two flashes of brilliance – Madras 1985, Bridgetown 1994, Adelaide 1995, Edgbaston 1997 – to sustain the illusion of light at the end of the tunnel. But more often than not power failure would strike just at the wrong moment, leaving a nation to wonder whether the gloom would ever lift.

Working parties were set up with earnest regularity to try to unearth some deeper malaise, but little improved. By 1994–5 England were regularly losing the Ashes, which is the only series that has any resonance with the floating British sports fan. Writing in *Wisden*, the editor Matthew Engel noted: "England

Steve Harmison completes figures of seven for 12 in the first Test against West Indies at Sabina Park in Kingston, Jamaica March 2004

LEFT Jacques Kallis, South Africa's middle-order rock, plucks another stroke from the coaching manual against England in Cape Town. January 2005

were beaten so badly in Melbourne that one sensed the Australians starting to regard the whole country, not just its cricketers, as a laughing-stock."

This state of affairs continued until the appointment as captain of Nasser Hussain in 1999, then Michael Vaughan in 2003, with their Zimbabwean coach Duncan Fletcher providing the common thread. Hussain got rid of the culture of defeatism, before Vaughan – a gentler character but no less determined for it – instilled the winning habit. Australia's world-record sequence of 16 Test wins a few years earlier had impressed with its sheer remorselessness, but then Australia have more often than not had a successful cricket team. The winning run of Vaughan's England sent shockwaves through a cricketing world which had long become anaesthetised to the buzz of humbling the mother country. When England beat South Africa in the first Test at Port Elizabeth just before Christmas 2004 it was their eighth win in a row, surpassing a national record last set in 1929. Had they not been so shocked, the players from 75 years earlier might have been turning in their graves.

One of the ingredients of England's new success was a strict adherence to a fitness regime which would have been laughed out of the dressing-room – any dressing-room – 15 years earlier, but which these days is taken for granted everywhere. It was a tradition among Australian touring parties to England to sink as many cans of beer on the plane on the way over as possible. The hard-partying wicketkeeper Rod Marsh was the early pace-setter, but David Boon – whose

equally squat physique made him the ideal receptacle – passed his record in 1989 with a grand total of 57 tinnies.

Boon somehow made it through customs, but these days he might not have made it past the first gym bleep test. Characters like the Australian middle-order batsman Darren Lehmann, who enjoys a fag and a pint at the close of play, are now looked upon as a throwback to more sociable – or possibly more rounded – days. But increased media scrutiny, the establishment all over the world of cricket academies and a more punishing schedule have meant that wobbly bits are frowned upon nowadays. To be an international cricketer in the 21st century is to subscribe to a fitness-first school of bench presses and Pilates.

For fast bowlers, it has become a case of do or die. The introduction of the ICC's 10-year schedule in February 2001 suddenly meant that teams were playing all year round, or at least felt like they were doing so. The new plan stated that every Test nation had to play the other nine in home and away series of at least two matches across each five-year period. The formalisation of the Test calendar made sense: it provided the longer version of the game with a structure it had always lacked and which could not be solved, for obvious logistical purposes, by a quadrennial World Cup-style jamboree.

The batsmen hardly cared about the crammed itinerary, because the more boundaries they could flog off tired bowlers, the less they would have to run

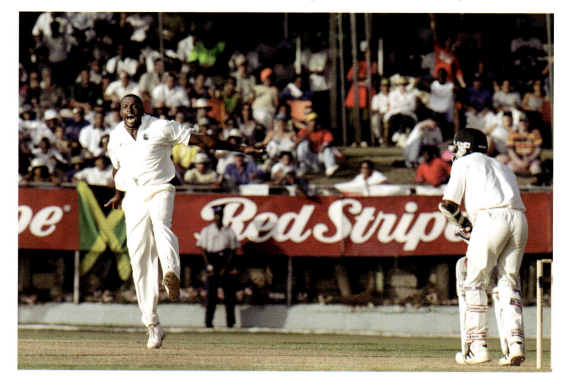

Courtney Walsh is ecstatic after breaking Kapil Dev's world record of 434 Test wickets in front of his home crowd in Jamaica – no matter that the batsman is the Zimbabwean rabbit Henry Olonga. Walsh went on to take 519 wickets before retiring in 2001.
March 2000

anyway. But injuries began to affect the fast men, even as medical care reached new heights. In 2003, England used 11 different new-ball combinations in 13 Tests, while India's epic draw in Australia in 2003–4 lost a bit of its gloss because Glenn McGrath – the most consistent fast bowler of the last 15 years – was absent injured. The flip side of this was that, as bowlers grew more tired and pitches flattened out, scores got bigger and bigger.

Of the 19 individual innings of 300 or more in Test history, seven have been made since the start of 1990. And in seven heady months from the end of 2003, the world record pinballed from Brian Lara (whose 375 v England at St John's, Antigua, had stood since April 1994) to Matthew Hayden (380 v Zimbabwe at Perth in October 2003) and back to Lara (400 not out, Test cricket's first quadruple-century, again v England, again at St John's, in April 2004).

Fourth-innings runchases were no longer approached with a fear bordering on paranoia. At Hobart in 1999–2000 Australia recovered from 126 for five to reach 369 for six and seal victory over Pakistan. In Antigua in May 2003 West Indies stuttered to 74 for three before chasing down a world-record 418 to beat Australia by three wickets and avoid a 4–0 clean sweep. And in the space of three games in 2004, England made 282 for three to beat New Zealand at Lord's, then hit 284 for six to beat them at Trent Bridge – records at both venues. Targets of over 200 were now regarded as a challenge, not a chore.

Some observers reckoned this was because the standards of bowling had dropped since the days when West Indian fast bowlers hunted not merely in pairs but in slavering packs. And yet the 1990s contained some of the finest new-ball pairings ever to play the

Dinesh Karthik performs acrobatics to ensure that the England captain Michael Vaughan is out stumped off Harbhajan Singh during India's consolation 23-run win over England in The NatWest Challenge at Lord's. September 2004

Wasim Akram, left, and Yousuf Youhana are delighted as the umpire Peter Parker sends Ricky Ponting on his way for 0 at Hobart. But Australia – as usual – went on to win. November 1999

game: Curtly Ambrose and Courtney Walsh of West Indies; Allan Donald and Shaun Pollock of South Africa; Glenn McGrath and Jason Gillespie of Australia; Wasim Akram and Waqar Younis of Pakistan. If the upcoming breed of quicks in the new millennium did not prove as consistently hostile – with the possible exceptions of Shoaib Akhtar and Steve Harmison – then it was probably because we had come to expect too much.

But then batsmen have not been making their lives easy. The former Australian captain Steve Waugh said that the Indian batting line-up which secured a draw down under in 2003–4 must have been one of the most dazzling in cricketing history – and few would argue against a side which included the flashing brilliance of Virender Sehwag and Sourav Ganguly, the wristy charm of VVS Laxman, the masterful solidity of Rahul Dravid and the all-round genius of Sachin Tendulkar.

The thing was, Waugh had a pretty handy collection in his own team. The muscular Matthew Hayden – more like a rugby-league forward than a Test opener – did what few had succeeded in doing since the retirement of Viv Richards in 1991 and actually intimidated the bowlers. Where Richards would stroll menacingly to the crease, chewing gum and preferring his distinctive West Indies cap to the safer but more anonymous helmet favoured by virtually everyone else, Hayden sought to impose himself by clumping some early boundaries over the top. Cricket had always been a psychological battle; Hayden was determined to win it from the outset.

Then there was Adam Gilchrist, the prototype for a new breed of uber-glovemen, who regarded their role as scoring quick runs as well as holding catches and pulling off stumpings. Others tried, but few could keep up with Gilchrist, whose murderously clean hitting at No 7 turned opposing bowlers to quivering wrecks. Until he belatedly replaced Ian Healy – a more classical wicketkeeper but a less feared batsman – behind the stumps for Australia in November 1999, an international keeper was expected to average around 30 and score perhaps four or five Test hundreds over a 10-year career. Gilchrist did not simply raise the bar: he hurled it out of sight.

Suddenly, the likes of England's Chris Read, or South Africa's Thami Tsolekile – skilled behind the stumps, less so in front – felt outdated. With Gilchrist trowelling the icing on a cake baked by Hayden, Justin Langer, Ricky Ponting, and the Waugh twins, Australia rarely settled for much less than four an over, a run-rate which 20 years earlier would have been regarded as a dangerous indulgence.

At times, Australia's desire to crush the opposition has not been universally popular. Their brand of verbal intimidation, practised with relish during the 1970s by Ian Chappell's team of moustachioed, open-shirted gunslingers, became known as "sledging", although, with a typically imaginative sleight of tongue, Waugh preferred to call it "mental disintegration". Since cricket is a mental game more than most, went the argument, why not exploit the fact by getting into the batsmen's minds? As a plan, it made sound tactical sense, but the repercussions were not always pretty and in 2003 the Australian board issued a warning to its players to behave themselves. It was one of the only flaws in a side that has stood comparison with any.

The one thing Australia really lacked was a world-class Test all-rounder. While their specialists continued to dazzle, this was no great problem, but it mirrored a wider dearth around the world. The 1980s had been spoiled for choice as Ian Botham, Imran Khan, Kapil Dev and Richard Hadlee kept a competitive eye on each other's progress.

Botham was the most destructive batsman, Imran the most glamorous bowler; but Kapil picked up 219 of his 434 wickets on the unforgiving strips of India, and Hadlee, the most elegantly incisive of the lot, played in a New Zealand team that gave him little back-up. The battle between Jacques Kallis and Andrew Flintoff still has a while to go to catch up.

"There was a lot of rivalry," remembers Botham when he looks back on the battle of the all-rounders. "Everyone would look and see who had done what round the world. Now it's a lot easier – you can go online and bang, there it is. Back in those days you used to wait for the papers or try to tune into World Service. If you were in New Zealand and someone else was in the Caribbean, you could be a day and a half behind."

Botham's reference to the internet is a reminder that the game has changed off the field too. For years the only live alternatives to actually being at a Test match were to watch it on TV or listen to it on radio. Then along came CricInfo, a website designed initially to allow fans to answer the game's favourite question: what's the score? No sport works as well on the internet as cricket, with its numerically definable moments and its constant stream of activity, and CricInfo quickly became the biggest single-sport website in the world.

Test matches as far-flung as Bridgetown and Brisbane might only be a click away, but that has not prevented the emergence of cricket's other major fan-centric phenomenon of the last few years: the Barmy Army. The rules are simple: follow the England team on every tour, sing lots and drink even more. Not everyone is impressed with the range of their lyrics or the harmony of their tunes, but the truth is that without the Barmy Army continually reminding us – as the song has it – who they are and where they come from, there would be a worrying lack of atmosphere at several Test venues around the world.

The game has moved on in the last 25 years, and the now-ritual appearance of the Barmy Army in cricketing cities throughout the world every English winter is just one sign of that. I know that the photos which follow will provide you with plenty more.

Happy place: the inimitable Adam Gilchrist has just bashed a tone-setting century in Australia's victory over India in Bangalore.
October 2004

Chapter One

The Domestic Game

In June 2003 a series of tremors shook the tranquillity of England's county grounds. The Twenty20 Cup had rumbled into town and immediately lived up to its promise of playing the party animal to the county championship's jaded wallflower. A crash-bang-wallop version of the sport packed into two-and-three-quarter hours and played in the early evening when fans were free to attend, Twenty20 made stunningly simple sense. Not only did it provide the perfect vision of how to bring the crowds back to the domestic game, but it also showed an exciting far-sightedness: here, perhaps, was a reason why county cricket might not wither away after all. Instant cricket had proved an instant hit, and national boards around the world pricked up their ears and whipped up their marketing men.

For too long the game below the highest level has faced a dilemma that can be summed up in three words: money, money, money. While international cricket has schmoozed TV companies and sponsors so successfully that no one-day tournament feels complete without a soft drink in its name and several hard-nosed logos on the outfield, the counties, states, provinces and islands face a perennial struggle to pull crowds and balance books. Understandably, they have thrown most of their eggs into a single basket: the one-day game, which attracts larger crowds, more TV coverage and thus a better class of sponsor than the first-class game.

How times have changed. Way back in 1981, when NatWest assumed sponsorship of county cricket's leading one-day knockout competition from Gillette, the thought of two teams going at it hammer and tongs for 20 overs each in front of big crowds was about as probable as England beating West Indies. Yet it is confirmation that, despite annual predictions to the contrary, the domestic game in the UK has stubbornly refused to die. Handouts from the England and Wales Cricket Board have been crucial, but as Twenty20 has demonstrated, the British public still regards cricket as an old friend – an attitude which has encouraged NatWest to pour more than £35 million into the game, much of it at grassroots level. And while NatWest have recently branched out into the international arena – with the World Cup, The NatWest Series, The NatWest Challenge and the first ever women's and men's international Twenty20 in the UK – it is lower down in cricket's food chain that a lot of their work has taken place. The NatWest Interactive Roadshow, which takes the game to the community, has become a familiar sight in towns and cities across the country, and more than 800 all-weather pitches have been distributed to schools and clubs. In an age when playing fields are making way for housing and hypermarkets, their 25 years of sponsorship and gospel-spreading have been increasingly crucial.

Other parts of the world have not always been so fortunate, though, and domestic set-ups have regularly stood accused of haemorrhaging the cash earned by the national boards. In 1986–7, the Shell Shield, at the time the name of the West Indies' inter-island first-class competition, had to be cut in half by the cash-strapped West Indies board, and had to rely on fresh impetus from new sponsors Red Stripe the following season to be restored to full strength. And in 1997–8, Australia's Sheffield Shield – later the Pura Cup – was incurring losses estimated at around A$6 million a year.

Tight purse strings have meant that national boards have had to tinker with the structure of their domestic game to try to strike a balance between preparing players for the rigours of international cricket and luring the punters. The Sheffield Shield/Pura Cup has usually led the way. In 1994–5 three venues introduced floodlit first-class cricket. A year later the six state sides were invited to choose their own nicknames, a move copied by the English counties in 1999. Gimmicks abounded. In a rare appearance for New South Wales in 1995–6 Steve Waugh earned A$140,000 by hitting

Record breakers: Gloucestershire's players celebrate winning the NatWest Trophy – their fourth one-day trophy in a row. August 2000.

England pack the slip
cordon on the final day
of their game against
the BCB President's XI
at the Bangabandhu
Stadium in Dhaka.
October 2003

Tom Moody of Western Australia onto a sign carrying the name of the one-day competition's sponsors.

Such attractions had relatively little success in persuading fans that state cricket was worth forking out for in an age of overexposure to Tests and, in particular, one-day internationals. Only in South Africa in the 1970s and 80s, when the country's cricketers were banned from the international stage because of apartheid, was the domestic game lapped up by spectators. Until the advent of Twenty20 it was left to New Zealand to carry out the boldest experiments. The first of these was Action Cricket, Twenty20's spiritual ancestor. Introduced in 1992–3, it was supposed to provide an antidote to one-day matches that lost their lustre when the side batting first was dismissed cheaply. Teams would play two sets of 20-over games, with a two-over slog deciding the winner if the score finished 1–1. Action Cricket lasted all of one season and Geoff Howarth, then the coach of Northern Districts, pointed out that "We've got too many who can bat for only 20 overs as it is." Soon they would have to bat only half as long: four years later, New Zealand's greatest batsman Martin Crowe came up with Cricket Max, a 10-over-a-

side whirlwind which began life with four stumps at both ends and encouraged batsmen to hit down the ground – the favoured area of the purists – for double the runs. Within a year an England side captained by Glamorgan's Matthew Maynard arrived in New Zealand to play a three-match Cricket Max series: the Max Blacks beat the English Lions 2–1, but Cricket Max never really found a place in the public's affections.

There were more orthodox means of drawing the crowds too. In 1987 Queensland signed Ian Botham in an attempt to win their first Sheffield Shield and put a stop to their status as Australia's longest-running sporting joke. For a while it worked. With Queensland charging only A$1 for admission – at times nothing at all – the crowds flocked to catch a glimpse of a man who had often held their national side to ransom. Unfortunately for Queensland, the wait for success would go on: it wasn't until 1994–5, at the 63rd time of trying, that they finally got their hands on the Shield.

For once, international cricket was elbowed out of the headlines, and just for good measure Queensland went on to win four Shields out of the next seven, including three in a row between 2000 and 2002 under the captaincy of Stuart Law. As reigns of terror go, it wasn't quite up there with the Surrey team of the 1950s, Bombay in the 1960s, Barbados in the late 1970s or the Transvaal "Mean Machine" of the 1980s, but Queenslanders, like starving men let loose at a banquet, were in no mood to be fussy.

Their pleasure suggested that the domestic game could engender passion after all, even if TV companies generally preferred the safer option of the international game. Sometimes the emotion went too far. In January 1991 West Zone's Rashid Patel attacked Raman Lamba of North Zone with a stump during the five-day final of India's Duleep Trophy, leading to a riot by the crowd and bans for the two players. But there were some touching moments too. When Sussex won their first county championship in 2003, at the 114th attempt, there was hardly a dry eye in Hove as the County Ground echoed to the club anthem "Sussex by the Sea". And though the championship was an easy scapegoat for brow-beaten followers of the England team in the 1980s and 90s, it remained the most evocative and well-supported first-class competition in the world.

Power ebbed and flowed. The 1980s were dominated by Middlesex and Essex, who lifted the title in 1983, 84, 86 and – after Worcestershire triumphed twice at the end of the decade – 1991 and 92. The middle of the 1990s, however, belonged to Warwickshire, where a magic triangle of captain Dermot Reeve, coach Bob Woolmer and record-breaking batsman Brian Lara helped the county to a unique treble: championship, Sunday League and Benson & Hedges Cup. Had they won the toss in the final of the NatWest Trophy, they would probably have pulled off a clean sweep. They were replaced as the team to beat first by a tight-knit Leicestershire, who used only 13 players to claim the championship in 1996 and 16 to win it in 1998, then by the all-stars of Surrey, who won three titles between 1999 and 2002. But Warwickshire had the last laugh in 2004 when their batsmen ground out a record 10 successive first-innings scores of over 400 and reclaimed the trophy.

The one-day honours were spread more evenly, although three teams stood out. Inspired by Viv Richards, Ian Botham and Joel Garner, Somerset won the B&H Cup in 1981 and 82 before lifting the NatWest Trophy the following summer. Next came Lancashire, who in 1990 became the first side to win both trophies in the same year, then repeated the feat in 1996. But Gloucestershire went one better, achieving back-to-back doubles in 1999 and 2000 and introducing the county game to their coach John Bracewell's idea of a claustrophobically attacking fielding unit. When they lifted successive Cheltenham & Gloucester Trophies in 2003 and 04 – NatWest's sponsorship ended in 2000

– they were rightly hailed as England's greatest-ever limited-overs team.

All the while, cries for reform of county cricket's structure grew louder, even though the three-day game, contrived finishes and all, had disappeared in 1992. The solution, hatched in time for the 2000 season, was to split the 18 first-class counties into two divisions of nine, with three up and three down at the end of each summer. Traditionalists bemoaned the potential loss of matches such as Yorkshire v Lancashire, but fewer meaningless games meant more competitive cricket, undeniably a good thing. What concerned the game's stakeholders more was the influx of cricketers into the county game who were not qualified to represent England. Bona fide overseas players had always been allowed in varying numbers. But when Maros Kolpak, a Slovakian handball player, persuaded the European Court of Justice in 2003 that he should be able to play in Germany without being classed as a foreigner because he already had a work permit, the county game faced the prospect of being legally obliged to accept cricketers from countries that shared trade agreements with the EU – including South Africa, Zimbabwe and parts of the Caribbean. The rumpus – peculiar to England because its season coincides with most other nations' off-seasons and because of its relatively large and fluid professional structure – typified the ever-present evolution that the domestic game must undergo to keep its paymasters happy.

Brian Lara has just become the first man to score 500 in a first-class innings. His innings of 501 not out for Warwickshire against Durham at Edgbaston came from just 427 balls and included 308 in boundaries alone. June 1994

The Remarkables mountain range forms a stunning backdrop as England take on Otago at Queenstown. March 2002

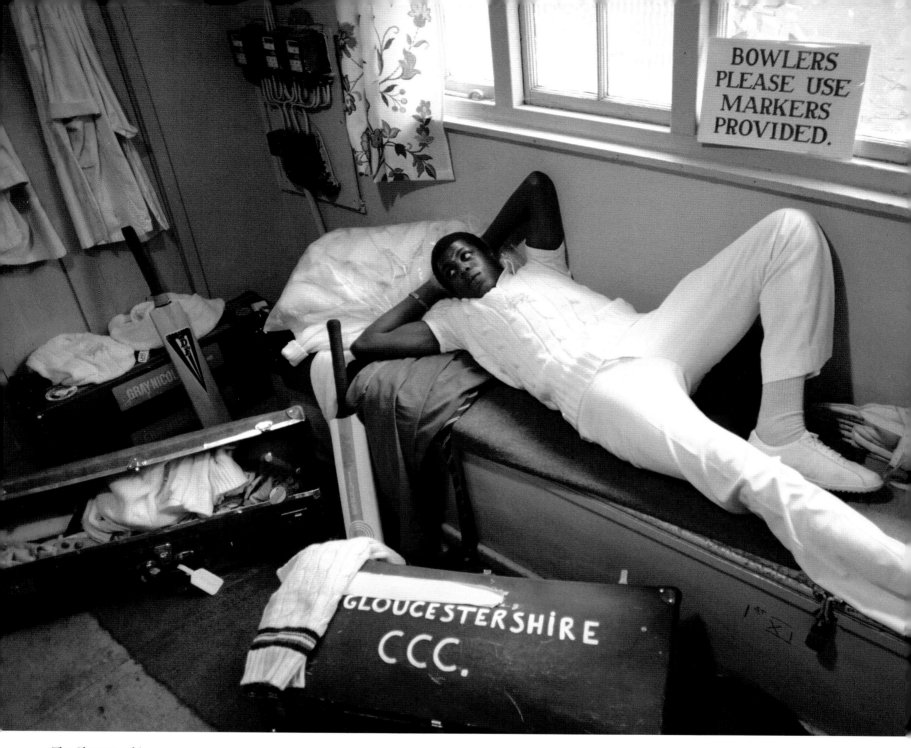

BOWLERS
PLEASE USE
MARKERS
PROVIDED.

The Gloucestershire
fast bowler Syd
Lawrence takes a
breather in the
dressing-room,
presumably while he
waits for his turn to
bat at No.11.
August 1981

The Waugh twins, Mark (left) and Steve, survey the scene during an ING Cup match for the New South Wales Blues against the Tasmanian Tigers at Sydney. February 2004

Warwickshire's Shaun Pollock jumps for joy after having Nasser Hussain of Essex caught behind for a duck with the second ball of the last-ever Benson & Hedges Cup final at Lord's. June 2002

Philip Weston celebrates his century as Worcestershire's Gareth Batty curses his luck during the final of the Cheltenham and Gloucester Trophy at Lord's. Gloucestershire won by eight wickets. August 2004

RIGHT A familiar sight as the maroon-hatted Richie Richardson square-cuts powerfully during an innings of 83 for the Leeward Islands against England at Basseterre in St Kitts. February 1990

A young scorer keeps
track at Chipembere
School in Highfield
near Harare in
Zimbabwe.
February 2000

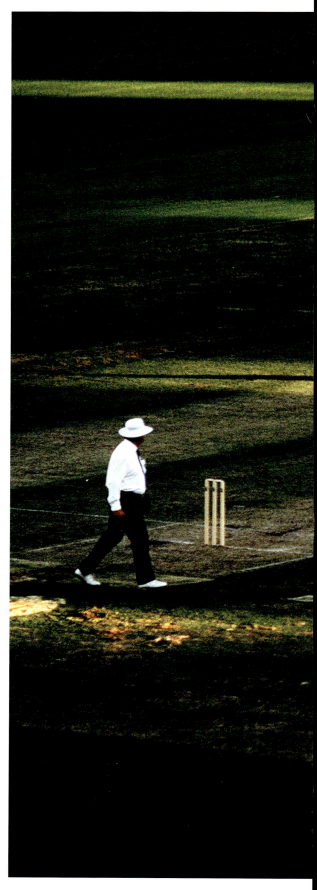

The shadows lengthen
over the Sydney Cricket
Ground as South
Australia's red-helmeted
batsmen turn for
another run against
New South Wales in
what was then known
as the Pura Milk Cup.
October 1999

LEFT All the caps are brown and the sky is grey as Surrey field against Lancashire in front of the Oval's evocative gasholder. April 2003

Ian Harvey flicks to leg in the Pura Cup final against Queensland at Melbourne. Victoria made 710 in their first innings on their way to a 321-run victory. March 2004

Graeme Hick is jubilant after helping Worcestershire to an eight-wicket win over Warwickshire in the NatWest Trophy final at Lord's. September 1994

Play continues in a third-grade game in Cessnock, north of Sydney, as a bushfire rages in the background. October 2002

A new season is about to begin but the only ducks on view at New Road in Worcester are of the feathered variety, after the Severn performs an annual ritual by bursting its banks.
April 1987

John Crawley strikes a typically languid pose while batting for England against Free State at Bloemfontein. November 1995

Shaun Pollock of Warwickshire keeps his eye on the ball during a net session at The Parks in Oxford. April 1996

Vasbert Drakes relaxes
during the drawn match
between the West
Indies Board XI and the
touring Australians at
St Kitts.
April 1995

The England A captain
Alan Wells waits for the
hail to stop before
leading his side to an
innings win over the
county champions
Warwickshire at
Edgbaston.
April 1995

Warwickshire's
Dominic Ostler takes
cover as Nasser
Hussain cuts during the
NatWest Trophy final at
Lord's. Essex stormed to
victory with more than
33 overs to spare.
September 1997

It's April in The Parks.
It must be freezing.
April 2003

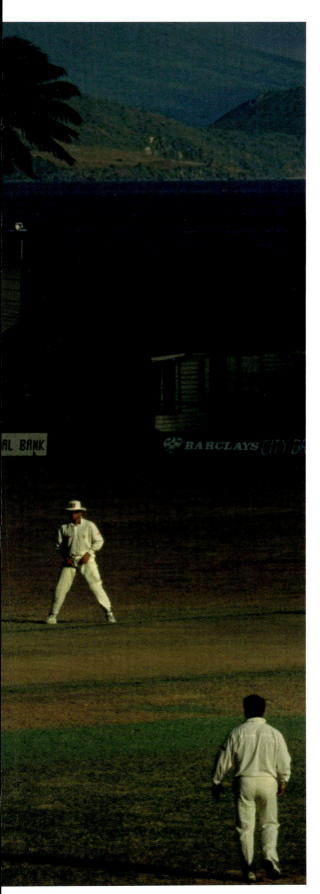

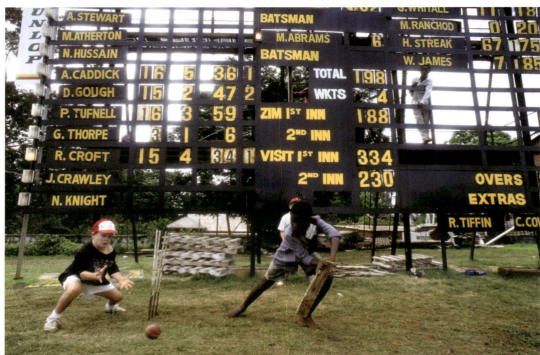

A young boy thinks about a quick single during England's tour match against Matabeleland in Bulawayo, Zimbabwe. December 1996

A cruise ship illuminates the background as the West Indies Board XI and Australia meander to a draw at St Kitts. April 1995

Members of the
Marylebone Cricket
Club – bacon-and-egg
ties resplendent – wait
for the Grace Gates to
open before the start of
another day's play
at Lord's.
August 2000

A DIY game of cricket
at Pearls Airport
in Grenada.
April 2003

Dougie Brown (left)
gets animated on the
Lord's balcony while his
Warwickshire team-
mate Allan Donald
contemplates life.
August 2000

Andrew Flintoff scatters
the pigeons during an
innings of 137 against
Surrey at The Oval in a
rare appearance for
Lancashire.
May 2002

Cambridge University's Vikram Kumar wonders what might have been after losing his wicket against Middlesex. April 2002

The New Zealand
batsman Mathew
Sinclair is not a happy
man as his side
crumbles against New
South Wales in a warm-
up match in Sydney.
November 2004

A batsman sizes up a
drive during the
Amacal'egusha village
tournament in Border,
South Africa.
December 2002

The shadows are about to encroach onto the wicket during the high-scoring Pura Cup draw between Queensland and New South Wales at the Gabba in Brisbane. October 2002

The former England
and Nottinghamshire
batsman Derek Randall
keeps himself amused
against Cambridge
University at Fenner's.
May 1989

The New Zealand
captain Martin Crowe
sweeps for four on his
way to 89 not out
against the Duchess of
Norfolk's XI at Arundel.
May 1990

LEFT Don't be fooled by
the Northamptonshire
cap: Kapil Dev is batting
against England during
their tour of India.
December 1984

Trent Bridge in
Nottingham basks in
the glow of a late spring
afternoon.
April 1998

Presumably the cricket isn't up to much in a county championship game between Warwickshire and Surrey at Edgbaston. August 2002

The South African
left-arm seamer Charl
Willoughby lets it go
during a match for the
MCC against West
Indies at Arundel.
July 2004

The Loughborough wicketkeeper Lee Goddard is at full stretch as Somerset's Michael Burns makes his ground at Taunton. Somerset made 840 runs during the match for the loss of just four wickets.
April 2003

The slip cordon is slightly overpopulated in a knockabout in Dhaka, Bangladesh. October 2003

The bowling action might be dodgy and the equipment rudimentary, but there's no shortage of enthusiasm in the streets of Rawalpindi, Pakistan. March 2004

Before the Indian Ocean tsunami turned it into a wasteland, the southern Sri Lankan resort of Galle was an ideal setting for a spot of beach cricket. February 2001

Adam Hollioake goes on
the pull as James Pipe
looks on during Surrey's
Twenty20 Cup victory
over Worcestershire at
The Oval.
July 2004

Mushtaq Ahmed, front,
leads a posse of Sussex
players waiting their
turn to bat against
Hampshire in the first-
ever televised Twenty20
match, at the Rose Bowl.
June 2003

The sun – or is that
the ball? – glows orange
as locals play on the
beach during England's
tour of Sri Lanka.
February 2001

The scoreboard
attendant at Fenner's
waits patiently for
the last Cambridge
University wicket to
fall in a game against
Middlesex.
April 2002

Chapter Two

The Tests

The Test match is one of the wonders of the modern sporting world. Not so much because of its drawn-out theatre, underscored by twisting subplots, flurries of action and engaging dramatis personae, although they are compelling enough. No, the real fascination resides in Test cricket's resilience. Because, in these consumerist times, anything that has "entertainment" on the tin but still lasts up to five days should really have reached its sell-by date long ago.

Yet the tale of Test cricket over the last 25 years is of a game that has not merely refused to die, but has been given a new lease of life, sometimes to the point where it has needed to step back and take a breather. More teams are playing more Tests at more venues than ever before. The batsmen are scoring faster, the bowlers are learning new tricks, and the fielders are throwing themselves around with increasing elasticity. Inevitably, the threat of player burnout – no longer a scourge exclusive to teenage tennis players – has become a major issue, and other controversies have raged like never before, from ball-tampering via match-fixing to chucking. But all the while the game itself has continued to fascinate, deflate and exhilarate, often in the same day.

The modern era has also been a tale of two empires: the rise and fall of West Indies, and the rise and rise of Australia. Pundits have tried to determine which of the two sides had the greater claim to being the best-ever: Clive Lloyd's West Indians, who won 11 Tests in a row between April and December 1984, or Steve Waugh's Australians, who trumped that with a world-record 16 straight wins between October 1999 and March 2001. It was a bit like leaving the irresistible force and the immovable object together in a room, and coming back later expecting to find a winner.

West Indies based their dominance on a ruthless four-pronged pace attack, a tactic that had occurred to Lloyd some years before. In 1975–6, West Indies were thrashed 5-1 in Australia, with Jeff Thomson and his partner-in-speed Dennis Lillee taking 56 wickets at the ferocious rate of one every 30 balls. West Indies did not know what had hit them, and when India easily chased over 400 against their spinners to win a Test in Trinidad a few months later, Lloyd snapped. From now on, fast bowling was the answer. "I developed the killer instinct," he said, an epiphany that would draw wan smiles from opposition batsmen in the years to come. In the very

next Test in Jamaica Lloyd let fly with his quicks, and five Indian batsmen were recorded as "absent hurt" in the second innings. A new era was born.

But the key to West Indian success over the coming decade was not simply physical intimidation, even if more players retired hurt against them in the 1980s than against the rest of the Test nations put together. On top of that, batsmen were subjected to a Job-like test of patience. The West Indies quicks were not just fast – they were accurate too. It is no coincidence that the five leading run-scorers against them were either short, like Sunil Gavaskar and Allan Border (and thus able to sway out of the way of the barrage of short balls); technically solid, like Geoff Boycott; or just plain gutsy, like Graham Gooch and Steve Waugh. But most sides had no answer, and although the critics objected to what they regarded as a throwback to the dark days of Bodyline, the statistics were irrefutable. In the 1980s, initially under Lloyd, later under Viv Richards, West Indies played 82 Tests and lost just eight. And their only defeat in 20 series came at the very start of the decade in New Zealand, where the local umpires did not exactly cover themselves in glory. West Indies had become a sporting phenomenon, and it would need something special to knock them off their perch.

The most obvious threat came from Australia, but for much of the 1980s, they were struggling to stay

TEST RESULTS
1980–2004
Australia
P264 W125 L64 D74
Bangladesh
P34 W0 L31 D3
England
P276 W78 L100 D98
India
P202 W49 L58 D94
New Zealand
P181 W46 L62 D73
Pakistan
P201 W75 L51 D75
South Africa
P122 W56 L28 D38
Sri Lanka
P147 W37 L57 D53
West Indies
P224 W87 L68 D69
Zimbabwe
P75 W8 L42 D25

Figures include any Test that began in 1980 and finished before the end of 2004. They do not include the tied Test between India and Australia at Madras (now Chennai) in September 1986.

Geoff Boycott is stunned after being bowled for a duck by the final ball of a Michael Holding over at Bridgetown. Most observers reckoned it was one of the finest overs in Test history. March 1981

afloat. Their nadir came during a sequence of three wins in 32 Tests between March 1984 and December 1986, during which their captain Kim Hughes resigned in tears. But his departure triggered the arrival of Border, who after several hiccups began to mould the team in his own tough-as-teak image. Never was his blueprint more clear than during the tied Test against India at Madras in September 1986, when Border taunted Dean Jones, who was vomiting regularly on his way to an epic double-century in sauna-sweltering conditions. "You weak Victorian," he said. "I want a tough Australian out here. I want a Queenslander." Jones remained at the crease before heading for hospital and a saline drip. But no one was left in any doubt: the path to the top would be long and occasionally hazardous.

Catharsis came for Australia when they lifted the 1987 World Cup, and sheer relief when the Ashes were regained in 1989. But West Indies would not budge. Australia lost 2–1 in the Caribbean in 1990–1, and then

came within two runs of their first series win over them for 17 years at Adelaide in January 1993, when Craig McDermott was agonizingly caught behind off Courtney Walsh after adding 40 for the last wicket with Tim May. The tide, though, was turning, and West Indies's increasingly fragile impressions of King Canute finally came to an end in Jamaica in May 1995. With the series all-square at 1–1 going into the fourth and final Test, Australia romped home by an innings and 53 runs, thanks to a stand of 231 between the Waugh twins – Steve made a Test-best 200, Mark 126. By now the captaincy had passed from Border, who had retired over a year earlier with a world-record 11,174 Test runs, to Mark Taylor, an affable left-handed opener from Wagga Wagga in New South Wales, whose ample embonpoint merely added to the feeling that here was a fair dinkum bloke who had somehow stumbled across life as an international cricketer.

In fact, Taylor was as competitive as the next Aussie and determined not to waste the legacy bequeathed by

Border. If Border had put the steel back into Australian cricket, making them the toughest side in the world, Taylor added a touch of gold by turning them into the best. Under his intelligent leadership Australia won 11 series out of 14, faltering only in the subcontinent. If there was a failing, it was, typically, a likeable one: Taylor could not quite bring himself to be ruthless, and on four occasions his side lost the last game of a series that had already been won. But that is to nitpick, and by the end of the 1990s the rest of the world was tearing its hair out.

Australia's evolution, though, was not complete, and it needed the remorseless Steve Waugh to take them to another level. After a modest start to his reign (a draw in the Caribbean followed by defeat in Sri Lanka), he led Australia on an unprecedented run of 16 victories (Taylor, remarkably, had never won more than three games in a row). It helped that Waugh presided over some of the most talented cricketers in the history of the game: a side containing players like Shane Warne, Glenn McGrath, Jason Gillespie, Matthew Hayden, Ricky Ponting, Adam Gilchrist and Waugh himself was as much a hall of fame as a cricket team. But a captaincy record of 41 wins in 57 Tests marked him out as one of the all-time greats.

It was almost as much of a compliment to say that Australia's rise to power had helped change the way Test cricket was played. The beguiling success of Warne – leg-break, flipper, zooter, you name it – brought spin bowling back to life after the pace-dominated 1980s. No one denied that all the best teams contained one or two genuinely fast bowlers. But suddenly everyone wanted what the former England captain Nasser Hussain would wistfully refer to as a "mystery spinner" – a bowler who could not merely think outside the box, but pluck magic tricks from it too. When Warne conjured up that delivery to bowl Mike Gatting in 1993, it was open season on sorcery.

Predictably, Warne's greatest rivals came from the subcontinent, where the turning ball was a way of life. India's Anil Kumble sent down nagging top-spinners at almost medium-pace, and became only the second bowler, after England's Jim Laker in 1956, to take all 10 wickets in a Test innings, against Pakistan at Delhi in February 1999. Muttiah Muralitharan of Sri Lanka ostensibly bowled off-spin, but such was the tweak he imparted on the ball that his action defied classification as much as it courted controversy. And, like Murali, both Saqlain Mushtaq of Pakistan and India's Harbhajan Singh added the lethal "doosra" (Hindi for "second" or "the other one") to their repertoire – the off-spinner's leg-break, and often unreadable. And the good old off-break? That was so 1980s.

Australia's impact could be felt in the batting too. At a coaching conference in Birmingham in 1999, Bob Woolmer, then the coach of South Africa, said that teams needed to score at 2.80 runs per over to win Tests. Steve Waugh's side begged to differ, and by 2003 Australia were galloping along at 4.08 an over. The difference in the course of a single day of 90 overs was 115 runs, which gave the faster-scoring sides more time to dismiss their opponents twice. Australia were making the hard-fought draw look like a dusty relic, and at one point Waugh was even championing the cause of four-day Tests. You could see where he was coming from: of the seven draws he presided over as captain, only two were not affected by the weather. His message caught on, even if it was helped by increasingly bland pitches and back-to-back Tests that played into batsmen's hands by reducing the fast bowlers' impact. But research in Australia at the end of last year revealed that seven of the 15 fastest scorers in Test history were still playing the game. Don Bradman came in a lowly 16th.

But while Waugh's unrivalled armoury meant he could afford to reach for the stars, other sides had to be more pragmatic and settle for terra firma. England, in particular, spent almost two decades in no-man's land before Hussain and Michael Vaughan found their bearings. The 1980s provided morsels to chew on for England fans – particularly against Australia – but not even world-class players like Ian Botham, David Gower or Graham Gooch could distract from the unpalatable truth: England no longer belonged on Test cricket's top table. They won only 20 and lost 39 of their 104 Tests in the 1980s, plumbing the depths in 1988 when they appointed four captains for the five-Test series at home to West Indies. Between them, Gatting, John Emburey, Chris Cowdrey and Gooch scraped a single draw, which at least represented an improvement on England's two previous meetings with West Indies: both had ended in 5–0 drubbings.

The 1990s occasionally hinted at renaissance as England won 26 Tests out of 107, but they still lost 43 games, not to mention three captains: Gooch and Mike Atherton resigned, while Alec Stewart was unfortu-

Steve Waugh (left) and Jason Gillespie recover in hospital after colliding in the outfield at Kandy in Sri Lanka. Waugh broke his nose while Gillespie fractured his right leg and left wrist. September 1999

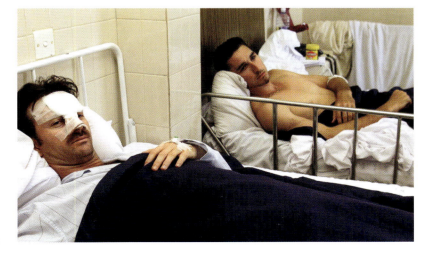

Jack Russell readies his gloves more in hope that expectation as Kapil Dev swings Eddie Hemmings for a fourth successive six to save the follow-on at Lord's. But it merely postponed the inevitable: England, inspired by 456 runs in the match from Graham Gooch, beat India by 247 runs. July 1990

nate to be sacked within a year of leading them to their first major series win for 12 seasons against South Africa. Hussain took over in 1999, but things got worse before they got better. England lost 2–1 at home to an under-rated New Zealand side, and plummeted to the bottom of *Wisden*'s unofficial world ratings, below even Zimbabwe. The consensus in the tabloid press was clear: English cricket RIP.

Then along came Duncan Fletcher, a Zimbabwean who two summers earlier had led Glamorgan to their first county championship title for 27 years, and whose phlegmatic features belied an acute mind. Fletcher's first act as coach was to watch England slump to two for four against South Africa at Johannesburg, but a steady, practical hand on the tiller and an eye for talent, combined with Hussain's burning intensity, gradually turned England round. The following summer they beat West Indies for the first time in 31 years, and then won in both Pakistan and Sri Lanka in the winter of 2000–1. Eighteen months after fighting back the tears after the New Zealand debacle, Hussain was being hailed as England's best captain since Mike Brearley. When the relatively sanguine Vaughan took over in

July 2003 the culture of defeatism was a thing of the past. He led England to their first series win in the Caribbean for 36 years, then oversaw seven wins out of seven in the summer of 2004. Cricket was on the back pages again, with Steve Harmison and Andrew Flintoff vying for space with David Beckham and Wayne Rooney.

England's overall sequence of 10 wins in 11 games was spoiled only by Brian Lara. Ten years after hitting what was then the highest individual score in Test cricket – 375 against England at Antigua – Lara was at it again, this time crafting an almighty 400 not out at the same venue to reclaim the record he had lost to Matthew Hayden (380 against Zimbabwe at Perth) seven months earlier. It was a rare moment of relief for a West Indies side that had badly lost its direction since being toppled by Australia. Nowhere was their decline more evident than in their record outside the Caribbean: 25 wins out of 52 in the 1980s; 11 out of 40 in the 1990s; and, after defeat at The Oval in September 2004, five wins out of 30 in the 2000s, four of them against the whipping-boys Zimbabwe and Bangladesh. The odd vignette from Lara every now and then was not enough to dissuade the West Indies board from taking drastic action, and in October 2004 they appointed the Queenslander Bennett King as their new coach – their first from outside the Caribbean and as such a cry for help.

In fact, West Indies had been slow off the mark. Foreign coaches had been the rage for a few years as teams sought to inject freshness into set-ups that had become stuck in the mud. India, who in late 2000 appointed the former New Zealand opener John Wright, and Pakistan, who twice experimented with the South African-based, English-born Richard Pybus before settling on Woolmer in July 2004, were cases in point: the first a sleeping giant, the second veering alarmingly between bouts of hyperactivity and somnambulism, with spells of infighting thrown in just to keep everyone on their toes. India's problem was that, for all the brilliance of their batsmen, they couldn't win outside the subcontinent: after winning in England in 1971, their only other success came in 1986, again in England. On the dry, dry grass of home it was a different story: between their defeat by Pakistan in 1986–7 and the loss to South Africa in 1999–2000, India went 11 full series without losing. But it was not until Sourav Ganguly took over as captain in November 2000 that India added flintiness to their repertoire.

Ganguly came from aristocratic stock in Calcutta, and upset some with his perceived haughtiness, but he was not afraid to get down and dirty either, especially when it came to taking on Steve Waugh. The 2000–1 series between the two sides was one of the most captivating in history. One–nil down in the three-Test series, India then won in Calcutta after following on, thanks to 281 from VVS Laxman, who added 376 with Rahul Dravid, and 13 wickets in the match for Harbhajan. In the decider at Chennai, Harbhajan Singh did even better, taking 15 wickets as India pulled off a thrilling two-wicket victory. Three years later the sides met again, this time in Australia, where India's notoriously fragile travellers had never won a series. In the end they had to settle for a thrilling draw after taking the lead at Adelaide. But Indian excitement at holding the Aussies on their own turf was cut short when Australia popped in at the end of 2004 and turned the tables with a 2–1 win. It was Australia first's win in India for 35 years.

The hype generated by the India–Australia encounters showed that times were changing. India still regarded Pakistan as the old enemy, but a political and territorial dispute over Kashmir meant that the sides played only three Tests between December 1989 and March 2004. Since 16 of previous 17 games had finished in bore draws, some would say that was no great loss. There was now almost as much frisson when India met Australia, who in turn were starting to look elsewhere for their thrills after eight successive series wins over their own traditional rivals England. And yet Pakistan's recent record is better than India's. From 1980 to November 2004, both sides played nearly 200 Tests: Pakistan won 75 and India just 46. In the 1980s, Pakistan were the only team consistently to give West Indies a game. And in the early 1990s, when they were in the mood, they were the most dangerous side in the world, thanks mainly to Wasim Akram and Waqar Younis, who moved the fast-bowler's line of attack from the ribcage to the toes. It was goodbye bouncer, hello yorker, particularly once the ball had lost its shine. The Pakistanis called it reverse-swing; the English batsmen who were unable to handle it in 1992 reckoned it had more to do with ball-tampering. It was not the first such accusation. New Zealand's Chris Pringle, a mediocre seamer who finished his Test career with an average of 46,

Steve Harmison is so excited after having Tino Best caught behind for a duck at Kingston that he makes a complete mess of the high-fives. Harmison finished with seven for 12 as West Indies crumpled to 47 all out, the lowest total in their Test history.
March 2004

India's Anil Kumble is convinced he has trapped Abdul Razzaq of Pakistan plumb in front at Multan. It was India's first Test in Pakistan for almost 15 years, and they celebrated with an innings win.
March 2004

admitted that his figures of seven for 52 at Faisalabad in October 1990 had come after he had picked the seam – but only in response to what New Zealand regarded as underhand practices by the Pakistan bowlers. In 1994, Atherton, then captain of England, was fined for applying dirt kept in his pocket to the surface of the ball during the Lord's Test against South Africa, and then failing to come clean with the match referee. More recently, both Sachin Tendulkar and Dravid have been charged with interfering with the condition of the ball – in the case of Dravid by rubbing it with sugar-coated saliva courtesy of a cough sweet.

By that stage, however, cricket had more serious problems. In April 2000 police in Delhi said they had intercepted mobile-phone conversations which implicated the South African captain Hansie Cronje in match-fixing. For a while no one believed it, particularly not at home where he was revered for turning South Africa into the second-best team in the world. And he was a born-again Christian who wore a bracelet inscribed with WWJD (What Would Jesus Do?). But as details emerged, Cronje's reputation turned to mud. He had accepted thousands of dollars for passing on information to bookmakers and, much worse, agreeing to influence the outcome of Tests and one-day internationals. England's win at Centurion in January 2000, when both sides forfeited an innings for the first time in Test history, turned out to be the product of one of Cronje's deals: the bookmaker in question had asked only that the game should not end in a draw.

Cronje's own story descended into tragedy. After being banned for life he was killed in a plane crash

in June 2002. But what Cronje referred to as "his unfortunate love of money" was merely the tip of a match-fixing iceberg that in darker moments seemed capable of sinking the entire game. Stories began to creep out from every nook and cranny. Pakistan's Salim Malik received a life ban after the results were finally released of an investigation into claims by Warne, Mark Waugh and May that Malik had tried to bribe them to throw a Test. India's Mohammad Azharuddin and Ajay Sharma were also chucked out of the game, and a whole host of big names were implicated in the cash-for-information scandal, where players would supply a bookie with pre-match titbits about things like the weather, the state of the pitch and team selection. Cricket fans everywhere began to wonder whether what they were watching was genuine sport or simply an extended spin of the roulette wheel.

The issue of chucking presented another problem for the spectator: were the bowlers who were most fun to watch – the fastest tearaways and the canniest spinners – all operating within the laws of the game? Problems started when Muralitharan was no-balled seven times for throwing by the Australian umpire Darrell Hair in front of a crowd of over 55,000 at Melbourne on Boxing Day 1995. Murali protested his innocence, arguing that a congenital deformity of his right elbow – he was unable to straighten it fully – and a merry-go-round wrist made his action appear worse than it actually was. Tests by Bruce Elliott, a human-movement specialist based in Perth, cleared Murali of any wrongdoing in 1996, but the whispering campaign never stopped, and in 2004 Murali decided to undergo further tests to verify the legality of his doosra, which had scuppered England in December 2003. They revealed a bend of 14 degrees, well over the limit of five degrees laid down for spinners by the ICC. But other tests showed that Murali was not alone: according to one estimate, 99% of all bowlers' actions contained some kind of kink, and in November 2004 the ICC agreed to re-examine the whole issue with a

view to introducing a new threshold of 15 degrees, the point at which a chuck is said to become visible to the naked eye. It was the most decisive action yet over an issue that had last stirred emotions in the 1960s.

The repeated slurs on Muralitharan's action obscured Sri Lanka's remarkable rise in the game in the 1990s. After making their Test debut against England in February 1982, they played only 28 more games before the end of the decade, winning just two. But they won the same percentage of their matches in the 1990s as New Zealand (21% – a figure that was only three fewer than that of England, who refused to play more than a single Test against them until 2000–1), and in 2001–2 won nine Tests in a row. Contrast that with New Zealand, who had to wait 26 years for their first Test win, or Bangladesh, who took 32 matches, and Sri Lanka had pulled off quite an achievement.

As 2004 neared its end, the boundaries between the Test nations were becoming increasingly blurred. Australia were way out in front at the top of the ICC's Test Championship, with Bangladesh and Zimbabwe, who were briefly stripped of Test status in 2004 because of the ongoing dispute between players and officials, adrift at the bottom. But England, Pakistan, India, Sri Lanka, South Africa and New Zealand were never more than a couple of wins away from swapping places with each other, and of the traditional power-houses only West Indies were in danger of losing touch. In the mid-table melee virtually every Test was up for grabs. And that is precisely how it should be.

Mushfiqur Rahman can smell victory as he and Javed Omar walk off for tea on the fourth day of the first Test against England at Dhaka. But the following day a relieved England completed a seven-wicket win.
October 2003

Pakistan's Saqlain Mushtaq adopts the pose after ending Dominic Cork's resistance on the final evening at Old Trafford. England lost eight wickets after tea to throw away the chance of a fifth series win in a row.
June 2001

Paul Adams's left-arm wrist-spin was once described as resembling "a frog in a blender". Here he lets another one go for South Africa against England at Lord's.
August 2003

It is not immediately apparent, but Darren Gough manages to keep his head while getting out of the way of a Curtly Ambrose bouncer during the Lord's Test against West Indies.
June 1995

Brett Lee's momentum carries him through the crease and past Sachin Tendulkar during Australia's thrilling draw with India at Sydney – Steve Waugh's final Test.
January 2004

Alec Stewart's reflexes are tested by Wasim Akram in the third Test at The Oval. Stewart hit 44 and 54, but Pakistan won the match by nine wickets – and with it the series.
August 1996

You wouldn't have guessed it, but Angus Fraser has just taken 11 wickets for England against West Indies at Port-of-Spain. The only problem is, West Indies have just won the Test by three wickets. February 1998

Graham Gooch's wince
confirms that his hand
is broken after it was
struck by the West
Indies fast bowler Ezra
Moseley in the third
Test in Trinidad.
England had been set
for a 2–0 lead, but the
game is drawn and the
series eventually lost.
March 1990

Mike Atherton sways dramatically out of the way of a smell-the-leather delivery from Courtney Walsh during a ferocious spell at Kingston.
February 1994

In the last of his 98 Tests, Curtly Ambrose drapes a brotherly arm over the shoulder of his faithful new-ball partner Courtney Walsh at The Oval. The pair would eventually retire with a combined total of 924 Test wickets.
September 2000

The New Zealand
captain Stephen
Fleming is lost in
thought as he sits in the
Long Room at Lord's.
New Zealand lost that
Test by seven wickets
after Nasser Hussain
finished his Test career
with an unbeaten
century.
May 2004

Mark Richardson is about to make a hash of things during the second Test between New Zealand and India at Hamilton. It didn't matter: New Zealand won by four wickets after both sides had been dismissed for under 100 in their first innings – a unique occurrence in Test cricket.
December 2002

Jolly Beach in St John's, Antigua, seems an appropriate place for the Australian squad – Baggy Greens and all – to show off the Frank Worrell Trophy after a 3–1 win over West Indies.
May 2003

Craig McDermott looks
as if he wants to hug
Asanka Gurusinha after
having him caught
behind for seven during
Australia's innings
victory over Sri Lanka
at Perth.
December 1995

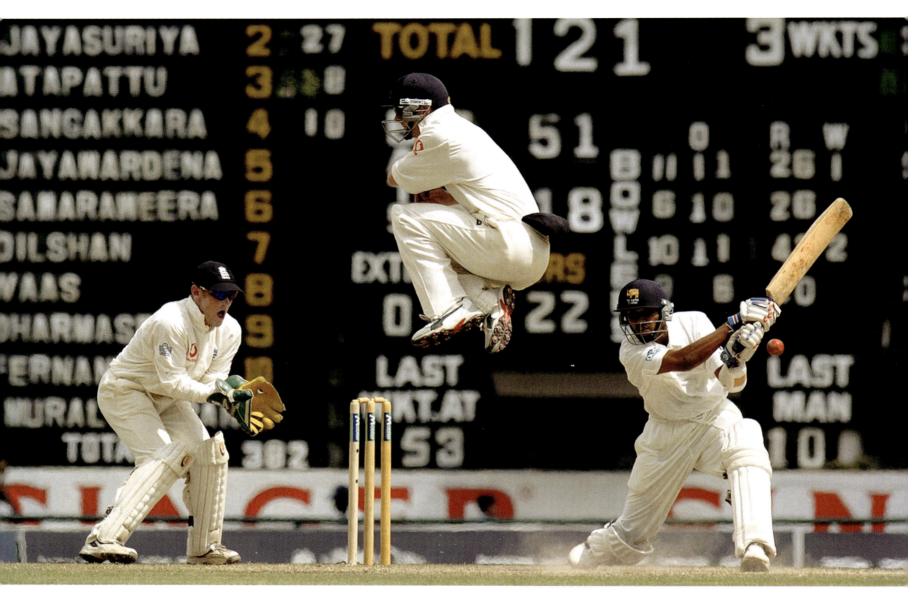

Chris Read is open-mouthed as Tillekeratne Dilshan drives through the covers against England at Kandy on his way to a century. Paul Collingwood performs the levitation at silly point.
December 2003

Andrew Strauss's attempted sweep shot is just about the only thing that fails to work on his Test debut against New Zealand at Lord's. Strauss makes 112 and 83 as England win by seven wickets. May 2004

For the first time ever, a Test match is abandoned because of the state of the pitch. England were 17 for three against West Indies at Kingston when the umpires decided someone was going to get seriously hurt. Onlookers survey the guilty strip.
January 1998

When bad light stopped
play at Centurion Park
in Pretoria during the
first Test nobody was
quite prepared for the
lightning display
that followed.
November 1995

Brian Lara stares
glumly out of the Old
Trafford pavilion during
the fourth Test against
England. Lara makes a
scintillating 145, but
Dominic Cork's hat-
trick helps England to a
nervy six-wicket win.
July 1995

Sachin Tendulkar looks
suitably quizzical while
holding the wrong end
of the bat as he prepares
to play his 100th Test
for India, against
England at The Oval.
September 2002

RIGHT For the only time
in his Test career Ian
Botham is out hit wicket
when he fails to "get his
leg over", as one radio
commentator put it, after
trying to hook Curtly
Ambrose at The Oval.
August 1991

The Indian crowd are in
good spirits as ever, but
Australia went on to
silence them in the
pivotal third Test
at Nagpur.
October 2004

As if bowling to the Australians isn't bad enough, Zimbabwe's Blessing Mahwire has to clamber into the Sydney Cricket Ground's Brewongle Stand to retrieve another six during his side's nine-wicket defeat.
October 2003

Graham Gooch is made
to feel at home on
England's ill-fated tour
of India. They lost the
Test series 3–0, the first
time India had
whitewashed them.
January 1993

Brett Lee goes round
the wicket during
Australia's series-
clinching four-wicket
win against South
Africa at Cape Town.
Ricky Ponting's
unbeaten century
helped them chase
down 331 in the
fourth innings.
March 2002

Curtly Ambrose rarely
gave much away, but
something tickled him
during the fourth Test
against Australia at
Bridgetown. Ambrose
took five wickets to
help West Indies to a
crushing 343-run win
and an unassailable
2–0 lead.
April 1991

Matthew Hoggard puts
the slips cradle to a
more literal use
during the build-up to
England's 10-wicket
win over West Indies
in Jamaica.
March 2004

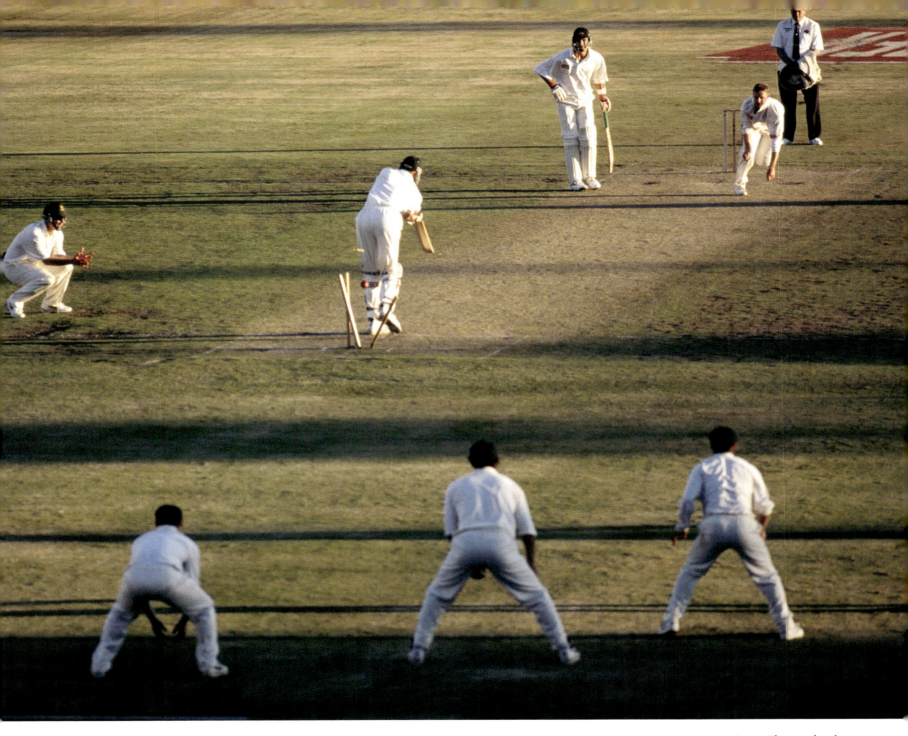

Lance Klusener bowls
Australia's Glenn
McGrath with the
penultimate ball of the
first day at Centurion
Park in Pretoria. South
Africa win by eight
wickets, but Australia
take the series 2–1.
March 1997

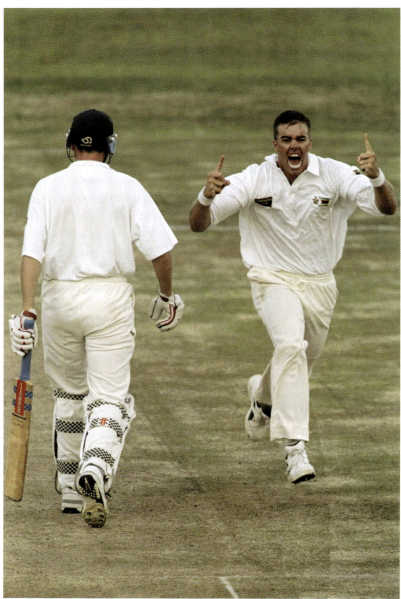

The India captain
Sourav Ganguly throws
back his head in despair
after narrowly failing to
run out Marcus
Trescothick during the
fourth Test against
England at The Oval.
September 2002

Heath Streak is jubilant
after having Mike
Atherton caught in the
slips for one during
Zimbabwe's draw with
England at Harare. The
series ended 0–0.
December 1996

Brett Lee demonstrates
why he chose cricket
rather than football
during the Antigua Test.
West Indies, 3–0 down
in the series, chased a
world-record 418 to pull
off the most satisfying
of consolation wins.
May 2003

The South African
captain Graeme Smith
celebrates his second
double-century in as
many as Tests against
England, this time
at Lord's.
August 2003

A flag flies at half mast at Wellington's Basin Reserve following the death of the England all-rounder Ben Hollioake in a car crash in Perth, Australia. Matthew Hoggard is the batsman trudging back to the pavilion.
March 2002

Alec Stewart sits in the dressing-room in Barbados, where he made 118 and 143 to help England become the first visiting side to win a Test there for 59 years.
April 1994

Fidel Edwards is caught
behind for a duck and
Andrew Flintoff has five
wickets for the first time
in a Test innings.
April 2004

Galle's 17th-century Dutch fort provides spectators with a bird's-eye view as Marvan Atapattu moves inevitably towards a match-winning double-century against England. February 2001

Left Darren Lehmann gets the full treatment during a drinks break on the fourth day of the first Test against Sri Lanka at Galle. Lehmann went on to make 129 to set up Australia's 197-run win. March 2004

Matthew Hoggard heads straight for the slips, where Andrew Flintoff has just caught Ryan Hinds to give Hoggard a hat-trick in the third Test against West Indies at Bridgetown. England won by eight wickets to move into a 3–0 series lead.
April 2004

Steve Harmison is convinced and his team-mates agree: Daryl Tuffey is caught behind for seven as New Zealand collapse on the fourth evening of the second Test against England at Headingley. The following morning, England wrap up the series.
June 2004

Mohammad Azharuddin has something on his mind during India's tour of England in 1990. Azhar averaged 85 in the series, but is best remembered for inviting England to bat first at Lord's, thus paving the way for Graham Gooch's 333. He was later banned for life for match-fixing.

Nasser Hussain lets out a roar of satisfaction after reaching three figures against India, the country of his birth, in the first Test at Lord's. Hussain's 155 sets up a 170-run win for England.
July 2002

Ricky Ponting has just mowed Paul Adams for six to bring up his own century and complete an astonishing win for Australia, who chased down 331 to beat South Africa at Cape Town.
March 2002

Michael Vaughan is in
pensive mood during a
net session ahead of
England's first Test
against West Indies in
Jamaica. England went
on to win the series 3–0,
their first victory in the
Caribbean for 36 years.
February 2004

RIGHT Life's a ball for
Steve Harmison as he
prepares for the first
Test between England
and West Indies at
Lord's. England went on
to win by 210 runs.
July 2004

The clouds are massing over The Oval in London during the fifth Test between West Indies and England. The rain eventually arrived on the fifth day, condemning a potentially exciting match to a draw. September 2002

LEFT It's that familiar jump and bent-arm gather, head tilted to the left, as Kapil Dev bowls during the third Test against England at Edgbaston. The game is drawn, but India take the series 2–0, a result which remains their most recent triumph outside the subcontinent.
July 1986

"The Turbanator" Harbhajan Singh dismisses Australia's Michael Kasprowicz during India's dramatic victory at Wankhede stadium in Mumbai.
November 2004

The picturesque surroundings of the Kensington Oval in Barbados during England's rain-affected draw.
March 1998

The England squad warm up for the second Test against New Zealand amid the old-world gentility of Christchurch. England were skittled for 82 and 93 on their way to a first-ever series defeat by New Zealand.
February 1984

Lumley Castle provides the backdrop as Zimbabwe's Heath Streak sends down the first-ever delivery in a Test match at Durham's Chester-le-Street to Marcus Trescothick. Streak picked up four wickets, but England won by an innings.
June 2003

Table Mountain towers over the Newlands ground in Cape Town, where South Africa are playing Australia in the second Test. The visitors win by four wickets to take the series.
March 2002

Darren Gough sinks to his knees after trapping Mark Boucher during the tense fifth and deciding Test between England and South Africa at Headingley. England won by 23 runs to pull off their first major series win for 12 years.
August 1998

Allan Donald described his tussle with Mike Atherton at Trent Bridge as the best 45 minutes of his career. Atherton gloved Donald to the keeper on 27, only for umpire Steve Dunne to give him not out, prompting a spell of frightening ferocity from the South African fast bowler. Atherton survived to make 98 not out and steer England to a series-levelling victory.
July 1998

Matthew Hayden
readies himself for
action ahead of the third
Test against Sri Lanka
in Colombo. Hayden
makes just 25 and 28,
but Australia win by 121
runs to complete a 3–0
whitewash.
March 2004

Alec Stewart is in no doubt about the way back to the Queen's Park Oval pavilion. Set 194 to win the match, England eventually stagger to 46 all out, their lowest ever total, with Curtly Ambrose taking six for 24. March 1994

Local children can
confirm that
Tillekeratne Dilshan
has just reached his
century against England
in the second Test
at Kandy.
December 2003

A scoreboard operator keeps an eye on proceedings during the first Test between Pakistan and India at Multan. March 2004

It's the end of an era as Dickie Bird administers one last leg-before decision before retiring as a Test umpire. The venue is Lord's, the bowler India's Sourav Ganguly and the batsman Jack Russell of England.
June 1996

LEFT Nasser Hussain bites his lip as he announces his resignation as England captain after the drawn first Test against South Africa at Edgbaston.
July 2003

Chapter Three

The Ashes

The concept of the Ashes began as a joke in a newspaper, but well over a century later the only laughter to be heard was emanating from Down Under. For much of the 1980s the Australians had come off second best in their biennial battles with England, but they readjusted their trademark Baggy Green caps, rolled up their sleeves and got down to the serious business of beating the Poms. They never looked back, except every now and then to laugh as another Englishman dropped a catch in the slips.

Eight Ashes wins in a row came their way, which equalled the all-time record set by England in the days of WG Grace, and Australia generally pushed their old rivals around as if they were prawns on the barbie. But if recent Ashes encounters have been little more than a case of Australia dishing out one thrashing after another – each one served with more relish than the last – then the fixture has somehow retained its unique mix of tradition and innovation, rivalry and affection, sportsmanship and gamesmanship, laughter and the occasional tear. England v Australia continues to stand the test of time as a concept, even if it has failed to do so as a contest.

It was back in 1882 that this grand tradition began. In a one-off Test match at The Oval England were cruising at 51 for two in pursuit of the 85 they needed for victory, only to fold to 77 all out after a devastating spell of fast bowling from Australia's Frederick "The Demon" Spofforth. The nerves were too much for one spectator, who was said to have chewed through the handle of his umbrella, while the frenzied climax proved literally heart-stopping in the case of another, who died of a coronary. The Sporting Times responded to the result by printing a mock obituary "In Affectionate Remembrance of English cricket which died at The Oval on 29th August 1882", and when England visited Australia later that year, winning 2–1, a group of Melbourne high-society ladies mischievously presented their captain Ivo Bligh with an urn containing the ashes of a ball, bail, or veil, depending on which version you believe. No matter what they were made of – they were about to become cricket's most treasured prize.

For much of the 20th century, the urn – or at least a replica of it: the original remained entombed in a glass case in the museum at Lord's – changed hands repeatedly, even if Australia had the edge. They held the Ashes for 19 years either side of World War Two, and then for 12 years until 1971. But when Australia arrived in England in 1981, they were the side trying to win them back. It remains a matter of some disbelief that they flew home that year empty-handed. For 1981 belonged to one man. These were Botham's Ashes. And Australians still wince at the memories.

The most resonant summer in English cricket's history had made a start that was more muffled drum than clashing cymbals. England were 1–0 down after two Tests, and Botham had resigned the captaincy after making a pair at Lord's, only to be told that he would have been sacked anyway. The new captain was the cerebral Cambridge graduate Mike Brearley, but when England collapsed to 135 for seven in their second innings at Headingley, still 92 runs short of making Australia bat again, they needed a miracle. They got Botham, freed from the yoke of leadership and playing once more with unfettered, to-die-for instinct. He famously informed his batting partner Graham Dilley that he was going to give it some "humpty", and true to his word slammed an undefeated 149 from 148 balls. Dilley somehow made 56, Chris Old hit 29, and

ASHES SERIES RESULTS
1980–2004
1981 England 3–1 (2)
1982–3 Australia 2–1 (2)
1985 England 3–1 (2)
1986–7 England 2–1 (2)
1989 Australia 4–0 (2)
1990–1 Australia 3–0 (2)
1993 Australia 4–1 (1)
1994–5 Australia 3–1 (1)
1997 Australia 3–2 (1)
1998–9 Australia 3–1 (1)
2001 Australia 4–1 (0)
2002–3 Australia 4–1 (0)

This table does not include the 1980 Centenary Test and the 1987–8 Bicentennial Test, when the Ashes were not at stake. Drawn games are in brackets.

LEFT **Ian Botham tests out Geoff Lawson's reflexes – and headgear – during the second Test at Headingley. June 1985**

RIGHT **Mike Gatting can't quite believe it after being bamboozled by Shane Warne's Ball of the Century at Old Trafford. It was Warne's first delivery in Ashes cricket – and left a scar that England's batsmen have struggled to heal. June 1993**

suddenly Australia required 130 to win. Shellshocked, they staggered to 111 all out, with Bob Willis – knees creaking, hair flying, eyes fixed as if in a trance – taking eight for 43 before haring from the field without so much as raising a grin. It was unclear who was more stunned: England, Australia or the bookmaker who had received a bet from the Australian fast bowler Dennis Lillee and their wicketkeeper Rod Marsh when the odds against an England win were 500–1. In an era before gambling on cricket matches took on more sinister connotations, this was the most prescient flutter in the history of the game. Only once before in 904 Test matches had the side following on gone on to win – and that was in 1894, when England shocked Australia at Sydney. But Botham was not finished yet. Not by a long shot.

In the fourth Test at Edgbaston, Australia had played themselves into another winning position, needing just 46 runs with six wickets left to take a 2–1 series lead. Enter Botham. His run-up to the crease was once compared by the broadcaster John Arlott to "a shire-horse cresting the wind", and now he galloped in like a Derby winner, taking five wickets for one run in 28 balls and giddying England towards a 29-run win. Next came Old Trafford and a century of such wilting ferocity that *The Times* wondered whether it was the greatest Test innings of all time. Botham hit six sixes – some off his eyebrows, one forcing the bowler Lillee to take cover as if faced by an oncoming missile – and 13 fours as he racked up 118 in 102 balls and left Australia an impossible target of 506 to stay in the series. They made a brave attempt but failed, and England retained the Ashes. Botham, meanwhile, took his place in cricket's pantheon.

Australia smarted for 15 months and then set about regaining the urn under Greg Chappell's leadership in 1982–3, when they saw off England by two Tests to one. But Australian cricket was about to go through what the team in question usually refers to as a

A rare champagne moment in the England dressing-room, where celebrations are under way after retaining the Ashes with an innings win at Melbourne. December 1986

transition period. It's the sort of phrase that has the opposition licking its lips, and England in 1985 were no exception. Since the win in 1982–3, three all-time Australian greats had retired: Chappell, Lillee and Marsh.

The side that now showed up in England had just lost successive series to West Indies and were captained by Allan Border, whose leadership experience extended to three Tests. For a while Australia held their own, but eventually England's string of big scores began to take their inevitable toll: in five of the six Tests England passed 450 in their first innings. The captain and new golden boy of the English game, David Gower, finished the series with 732 runs at an average of 81, and there were runs aplenty too for Mike Gatting (527 at nearly 88), Tim Robinson (490 at 61) and Graham Gooch (487 at 54). Botham, by now sporting a garish blond mullet and walking around as if he owned the place, chipped in with 30 wickets, and there were 17 in two Tests for the Kent swing bowler Richard Ellison, who helped England to a resounding 3–1 win with victory in the last two matches of the series at Edgbaston and The Oval. As Gower stood on the Oval balcony in the evening sunshine, holding aloft the urn in front of the cheering masses, Border plotted his revenge.

When it came, it would be fearsome. But for the time being it would have to wait. The reason England would achieve one more win on Australian soil – their fourth such victory since the war, but their last of the 20th century – was in no small part down to that man Botham and his first-Test heroics at Brisbane in November 1986. England's build-up to the Test series had been so disastrous that one wag in the travelling press corps had declared there were only three things wrong with the side: can't bat, can't bowl, can't field. Other than that, went the joke, everything was perfect. It was the sort of hopeless situation in which Botham thrived, and he immediately pushed Australia onto the defensive with a blistering 138 to set up a seven-wicket win. Two draws followed, before five wickets each for Gladstone Small and Botham, plus a century by Chris Broad – his third in successive Tests – sealed the Ashes at Melbourne.

For Australia, things could hardly get any worse: three defeats in four series against the mother country, culminating in a scarcely expected humbling in their own backyard. Their next visit to England would be in the summer of 1989, and Border decided that the only way to win back the urn was to play hard, both on and off the field. As he later told his opposite number Gower: "The last time we came here I was a nice guy who came last. This time I thought we had a bloody good chance to win and I was prepared to be as ruthless as it takes to stuff you." Presumably, the eventual score-line of 4–0 to Australia fell into that category. As far as

England were concerned, it was the start of the longest drought in modern Ashes history. And they only had themselves to blame. Their selection policy that year could be politely described as a complete shambles. In six Tests, they used no fewer than 29 players to the Australians' 12, and had the weather not intervened at Edgbaston and The Oval, they might well have been looking at only the second whitewash in well over 100 years of Ashes showdowns.

The difference in spirit between the two sides was tangible. While England regarded victory as their right after the triumphs in 1985 and 1986–7, Australia viewed it as a privilege to be fought for. Mark Taylor, the left-handed opener who would later become Australia's captain but who was about to make his first-

ever tour, revealed how he received a letter from the team manager Laurie Sawle prior to departure: "Congratulations on your selection for the 1989 Ashes Tour of England. We leave from Melbourne on the 29th April. We have a huge task ahead of us – to regain the Ashes. Australia has not won a full Test series [five Tests or more] in England since 1964, so there is quite a challenge ahead for the 1989 team. We need to start preparing for it now." Thanks to the apparently innocuous swing bowling of Terry Alderman, whose series haul of 41 wickets included an astonishing 19 lbws, and the coming of age of Steve Waugh, who made 393 runs in the series before he was even dismissed, Sawle's plea was answered in the most emphatic style imaginable.

**Hands up who thinks Kim Barnett has just prodded Terry Alderman to Dean Jones. England are 18 for two in their second innings at Lord's and heading for another defeat.
June 1989**

Shane Warne has visions of another bag of wickets ahead of the 1997 series in England. He finishes with 24 scalps at an average of 24.
May 1997

The zenith of Australian dominance came on the first day of the fifth Test at Trent Bridge, when their openers Taylor and Geoff Marsh walked off the field at stumps with the scoreboard reading 301 for no wicket. Taylor went on to make 219, an innings which prompted an over-the-top comparison in one English newspaper with Don Bradman himself. But perhaps the most damning indictment of England can be found in this revelation from the autobiography of Mike Atherton, who made his debut in that Trent Bridge fiasco as a rosy-cheeked 21-year-old: "One senior player said to me during the match, 'You play your first for love and the rest for money'." During the previous Test, at Old Trafford, it had been confirmed that several members of the England side had signed up for a rebel

tour to South Africa, thus theoretically forfeiting their right to play Test cricket for another five years. The senior player who confided in Atherton had merely summed up the broken, dispirited state of the England dressing-room.

The figures who would dominate Ashes cricket for the next 15 years were nearly all Australian. But some dominated more than others. It was time for Shane Warne. Australia arrived in England for the summer of 1993 having retained the Ashes with insulting ease on their own turf 30 months earlier. The talk was of a blond surfer who wore an ear-ring, swore a lot and spun the ball even more. Quite how far he spun it was not entirely clear until he sent down his first delivery in Ashes cricket on the Friday after-

noon of the first Test at Old Trafford. At the other end stood Mike Gatting, as brutal a player of spin bowling as any in the England side. Moments later he stood transfixed and open-mouthed, the victim of what most observers agreed was the Ball of the Century. Warne was no longer the slightly overweight beach bum of the tabloid imaginings: he was England's worst nightmare.

"In the second or so it took to leave my hand, swerve to pitch outside leg stump, fizz past the batsman's lunge forward and clip off stump my life did change," he wrote later. The psychological impact of that single delivery would be felt time and again in the years to come: if Australia's superiority was embodied in one man, it was in this cackling, probing, deeply gifted leg-spinner. In 26 Ashes Tests before the 2005 series, Warne had taken 132 wickets at an average of just 23. And his love of England batsmen was reflected by the fact that his five most frequent victims in Tests were all Poms: he had dismissed Alec Stewart 14 times, Nasser Hussain 11, Atherton 10, Graham Thorpe nine and Andrew Caddick eight. He did not merely eat them for breakfast, but for lunch and dinner as well.

And, with monotonous regularity, his team did the same to England. From 1989 onwards, Australia won 28 Tests to England's seven, only one of which came when the Ashes were at stake. That was at Edgbaston in 1997, when Australia crumbled to 54 for eight on the first morning of the series and Nasser Hussain cracked 207 to give a jubilant England an early lead. But it was the exception that proved the rule. When the initiative was there to be grasped, it was usually grasped by an Australian. Mark Taylor, by now the Australian captain, summed things up: "When Australia had its opportunity, the chance was almost always taken. With England, more often than not, the chance was not taken".

Seminal moments littered the Ashes landscape like dazed Englishmen. In 1994–5, for instance, Australia immediately strutted their stuff by racing to 26 without loss off the first four overs of the opening Test, and England never recovered. And in 1997, with the series in the balance at 1–1, Thorpe dropped Matthew Elliott on 29 at a crucial stage of the Headingley Test. Elliott went on to make 199, Australia won by an innings and another Ashes series would end in English disappointment. England could not even get their celebrations right. When Darren Gough took a hat-trick at Sydney in 1998–9, his team-mate Alex Tudor accidentally sunk his teeth into the back of Gough's head as he embraced him. Asked whether he would have any Englishmen in his starting line-up, Taylor had to be brutally frank: "None, but I'd take Gough as twelfth man to be around the dressing-room."

The era as a whole contained fleeting moments of relief for England: the sublime elegance of Gower, the devastating brilliance of Michael Vaughan, the never-say-die seam bowling of Angus Fraser, and the irrepressible chirp of Gough. But, depressingly for England, the gap between the sides was beginning to grow again and in 2001 Australia won for the seventh time in a row. "The Australians had taken the game on to a new level that summer," noted Atherton. "The aggressive batting of their middle and lower-middle order was the best that I had seen." From a man who had played in every series defeat since 1989, this was saying something. Atherton's own nemesis had come in the form of Glenn McGrath, a tall, metronomical seamer who developed the sort of love-hate relationship with Atherton that defined Australia's relationship with England: McGrath loved bowling to him so much that he almost hated to see the back of him. In all McGrath dismissed Atherton 19 times in Test cricket – a world record – and claimed a total of 117 wickets in 22 Ashes Tests, including eight for 38 at Lord's and seven for 76 at The Oval, both in 1997, and seven for 76 at Headingley four years later. England had no one to match his consistency. Indeed, their leading Ashes wicket-taker from 1981 onwards was Botham with 95 – and not one of those was picked up during the 1990s.

And yet victory over England continued to mean more to Australian cricketers than anything else, even with the hype that surrounded their epic series with India around the turn of the millennium. "For any Australian or Englishman," explained Warne in his biography, "the Ashes remains the most important series in world cricket, simply because of the history and tradition, the personalities involved in all the memorable battles of the past. It is the oldest series in the game and the one that neutrals always look to."

Michael Vaughan eases the ball past Matthew Hayden on his way to an epic 183 at Sydney. England's consolation win, by 225 runs, prevents the first Ashes whitewash for 82 years. January 2003

Jason Gillespie takes off after trapping a disconsolate Darren Gough lbw for a duck in the second Test at Perth. November 1998

Peter Such is caught and bowled by Stuart MacGill at Sydney via Michael Slater's boot at silly point, and Australia have won their sixth successive Ashes. January 1999

David Boon snaffles
Devon Malcolm at short
leg and Shane Warne,
on his home ground at
Melbourne, has
Australia's first Ashes
hat-trick since Hugh
Trumble at the same
venue in 1903–4.
December 1994

Glenn McGrath (centre,
holding sweater) is all
smiles after bowling
England out for 77
at Lord's.
June 1997

Simon Katich is full of poise as he rehearses his left-arm wrist-spin during the 2001 Ashes in England. Katich made his debut in the fourth Test at Headingley, scoring 15 and 0*.
July 2001

LEFT David Gower awaits another thunderbolt from Australia's tearaway Jeff Thomson in the second Test at Brisbane. Gower was one of five second-innings scalps for Thomson as Australia won by seven wickets.
November 1982

Marcus Trescothick takes
the aerial route against
Shane Warne at Brisbane.
But it was not enough to
prevent Australia
winning by 384 runs.
November 2002

Jason Gillespie can only grasp at thin air as Michael Vaughan drives on his way to 177 in the second Test at the Adelaide Oval. November 2002

Merv Hughes is on his knees as a stray dog stops play at Trent Bridge. Once back on two legs, Hughes takes five for 92. July 1993

Enemies on the pitch, Dennis Lillee (left) and Ian Botham are friends by the pool as they relax in Yalumba, South Australia. December 1982

The Australian captain
Allan Border can't bear
to look as he fluffs a
chance at Headingley in
1993. No matter:
Border's double-century
in the same game sets
up an innings win for
Australia and seals the
Ashes for another series.
July 1993

Marcus Trescothick is
down and out in Perth
against Brett Lee –
caught behind for four.
December 2003

LEFT Shane Warne sizes
up his next victim in the
second Test at Lord's.
He finishes the game
with eight in all.
June 1993

Michael Slater's
furniture is not so
much rearranged as
completely destroyed
by Devon Malcolm
at Sydney.
January 1995

The Sydney Cricket Ground erupts as their local hero, Steve Waugh, drives Richard Dawson's last ball of the second day through the covers to reach his 10th and final Ashes hundred. January 2003

It feels like Christmas
has come early for
Shane Warne and Merv
Hughes, who have just
shared 16 wickets to
get Australia off to a
winning start at
Old Trafford.
June 1993

A passing sun-shower
isn't enough to disturb
Damien Martyn's
concentration at
Headingley.
August 2001

The shadows are lengthening and the clock shows 6.10pm as the crowd runs onto the pitch to celebrate only England's second win at Adelaide since 1955. January 1995

The England captain Nasser Hussain takes on board some liquid refreshment ahead of England's hard-fought win at the SCG. January 2003

Matthew Hayden, on as a substitute fielder, performs acrobatics at short leg to get rid of Robin Smith for five at Lord's. Australia win by an innings.
June 1993

Craig White wishes he could turn back time after missing a sharp chance in the field at Edgbaston. The result? Another innings win for the Aussies.
July 2001

Mike Gatting serves
up the definitive cold
beer to his captain Mike
Atherton after England's
win in Adelaide.
January 1995

Elton John shares a joke with the victorious captain Mike Gatting after England retain the Ashes.
December 1986

The Australian Prime Minister, Bob Hawke, catches the mood of the Australian dressing-room. Dean Jones makes a point, while the captain Allan Border listens in.
June 1989

Fancy footwork isn't
enough as David Boon
collides with Phil
Tufnell at Melbourne.
Boon hits an unbeaten
94 in the second
innings as Australia win
by eight wickets.
December 1990

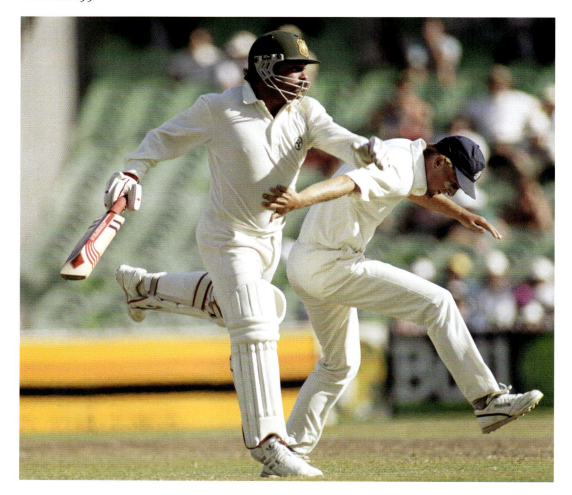

Graham Gooch bears
the scars of a faltering
Ashes campaign.
January 1991

Jason Gillespie is
ecstatic after trapping
Mark Ramprakash lbw
at Lord's. Justin Langer
provides the embrace as
Brett Lee moves in.
July 2001

Phil Tufnell allows
himself a hop and a
skip en route to match
figures of 11 for 93 to set
up an England win at
The Oval.
August 1997

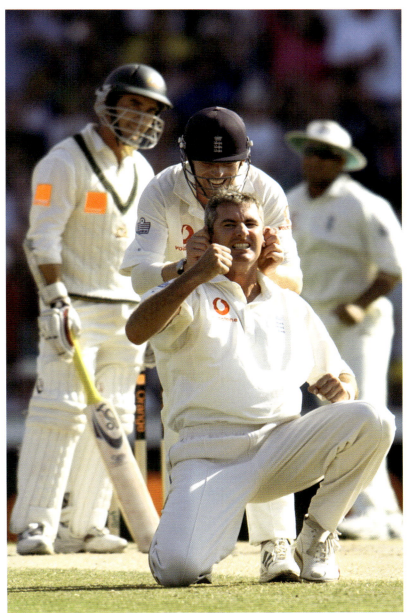

Andy Caddick receives
an earful from Richard
Dawson after trapping a
disbelieving Justin
Langer leg-before at
Sydney. Caddick's 10 for
215 inspired England to
a consolation win.
January 2003

The clouds gather over England at a packed Trent Bridge in Nottingham. Australia win the game by seven wickets and wrap up the Ashes for the seventh consecutive series.
August 2001

The England coach Keith Fletcher is a mixture of fury and resignation as he watches his side head towards a 4–1 series defeat in 1993.

Matthew Elliott pirouettes and pulls during his match-winning knock of 199 at Headingley. Elliott had been dropped by Graham Thorpe in the slips on 29 – another example of England failing to take their opportunities.
July 1997

The poetic partnership of Martin Love and Steve Waugh comes together at Sydney. January 2003

Less than three weeks after tearing a calf muscle, Steve Waugh hobbles his way to an unbeaten 157 in the fifth Test at The Oval. Even when he was on one leg, England couldn't get him out. August 2001

AUS
FIRST
Love
Waugh

Against the imposing backdrop of Perth, Mike Atherton takes the strain in Kings Park with the aid of England physio Dave Roberts and team-mate Mike Gatting. October 1994

A future generation of Australian cricketers waits to take the field during a lunchbreak at Adelaide. November 2002

RIGHT A sea of 60,000 sunhats soaks up the rays at the Melbourne Cricket Ground. December 1990

PREVIOUS PAGE There is something messianic about Ian Botham as he runs off the Headingley field after plundering 149 not out off 148 balls. Set 130 to win, Australia promptly tumble to 111 all out. July 1981

Steve Waugh and his inseparable Baggy Green cap. In all, he wore it 167 times for Australia – a world record for Test appearances. November 2002

So this is what all the fuss is about. Sport's most famous urn contains merely the ashes of a burnt ball or a bail or even a veil, but to the cricketers of England and Australia it means everything.

Chapter Four

The One-day Game

It was not the most dignified way to start a revolution. "Come on gentlemen," said Kerry Packer. "There's a little bit of the whore in all of us. Name your price." It was June 1976 and the gentlemen in question, members of the Australian Cricket Board's television sub-committee, had all but signed a new deal with the Australian Broadcasting Corporation to cover international cricket in their country for the next three years. But Packer, a bullish media magnate with a middle name – Bullmore – to suit, was on a mission. He wanted to secure exclusive rights for his own TV stations, TCN-9 Sydney and GTV-9 Melbourne, and was prepared to pay $A1.5m for the privilege when the ABC's contract ran out three years down the line. That was a vast sum in the 1970s, but the ACB were non-committal, and Packer left the meeting already planning his next move. "In that case," he thought to himself, "we'll just have to set up our own matches instead."

Like an incessant hypochondriac, cricket had usually imagined itself to be in the throes of a crisis, but this time the symptoms were genuine. Packer was not a man to be turned down, and now used his considerable charisma and financial clout to sign up some of the game's best players, including the cream of Australia and West Indies, and the England captain Tony Greig. While cricket establishments all round the world choked on their gin and tonics and spoke grandly of betrayal – others felt that they were merely being shaken out of their complacency and that the players would now get the money they deserved – Packer gave birth to World Series Cricket. It was a revolution that would change the game forever.

Packer's Supertests were one thing, but it was the one-day internationals which really upset the old order, and many of the gimmicks that the contemporary fan takes for granted were spawned by WSC: floodlights, white balls, black sightscreens, coloured clothing, even nationalistic jingles. Packer's detractors called the World Series a circus, and it is true that it lasted less than three years. But his entrepreneurial drive had shunted the entire game through the gears. Almost everything that happened in the one-day arena after Packer could be traced back to Packer himself.

Whether the traditionalists like it or not, the one-day international is now a fact of life. By the end of the ICC Champions Trophy in September 2004, a total of 2,182 ODIs had been played worldwide (and the abbreviation ODI had become a standard part of cricket's vocabulary). Appropriately for the blink-and-you-might-miss-it form of the game, it has travelled a long way in a short space of time. On January 5, 1971, the scheduled last day of the rain-obliterated Ashes Test at Melbourne, Australia, and England decided to put on a show for the spectators and TV cameras and bat for 40 eight-ball overs each to determine the winner of the first-ever limited-overs international. In front of a crowd of 46,000 England were inserted by Bill Lawry and dismissed for 190, with Geoff Boycott's eight off 37 deliveries highlighting the uncertainty in the players' approach. Australia then knocked off the runs with five wickets and five overs to spare. The second one-day international did not take place for another 20 months, when Dennis Amiss hit the first century to help England to a six-wicket win over Australia at Old Trafford, but other teams gradually began to take note. New Zealand met Pakistan at Christchurch in February 1973, West Indies played their first ODI in September 1973, and India joined the party in July 1974.

Includes all teams who played 10 or more games between the start of 1980 and the end of 2004

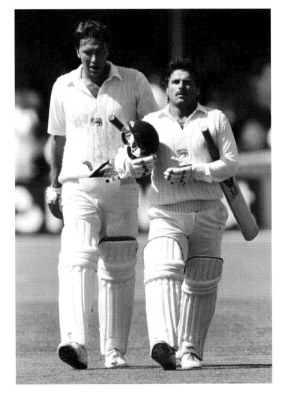

LEFT Andrew Flintoff hits out on his way to 123 as England take on West Indies at Lord's in The NatWest Series. But it is not enough to prevent defeat. July 2004

Allan Lamb (right) walks off with Derek Pringle after hitting an unbeaten century against Australia at Trent Bridge. The game finishes in a tie. May 1989

The game spread slowly, almost cautiously, at first, as if being careful not to tread on the toes of Test cricket, its more venerable, older sibling. It was not until December 1980, almost 10 years after the Melbourne experiment, that the 100th ODI took place. But in the post-Packer years the matches multiplied like frisky rabbits as national boards cottoned on to the huge amounts of money to be made, both at the turnstiles and from the TV companies. The 500th game was played in January 1988, the 1000th in May 1995, the 1500th in September 1999, and the 2000th in April 2003.

There were times, especially on the subcontinent towards the end of the 1990s, when you could barely turn on the television without coming across the latest round-robin encounter in some obscure competition sponsored by a soft-drinks giant in a part of the world with little or no cricketing heritage at all. In the space of seven months in 1999 and 2000, for example, Coca-Cola paid to have their name associated with the Singapore Challenge, the Champions Trophy in Sharjah, and the Coca-Cola Cup, also in Sharjah. Perhaps Packer's remark about everyone having a little bit of the whore in them was not so throwaway after all.

England's Norman Cowans runs out New Zealand's Warren Lees during a Benson & Hedges World Series Cup game at Melbourne. But New Zealand have the last laugh, winning by two runs despite a brilliant David Gower century. January 1983

One-day cricket might have started life as a bit of fun between the game's two oldest powers, but it was the newish kids on the block, India and Pakistan, who took to it with special relish. In 1998 and 1999, at the peak of their any-game-anywhere mentality, India played a total of 83 one-day internationals – one every eight or nine days; in 2000 alone, Pakistan played 41. When Pakistan met England at Cape Town during the 2003 World Cup, Wasim Akram was winning his 499th one-day international cap, which was 10 more than the entire England team, minus Alec Stewart, put together. The numbers were overwhelming. Between 1980 and the end of September 2004, Pakistan played a total of 574 ODIs. India came next with 561, followed by Australia, whose annual round-robin competition continued to be known for many years as the World Series, on 544. Of the established Test nations, England were way behind in seventh with 356, ahead of only South Africa on 318 – and they didn't play their first game until November 1991. The six leading wicket-takers in one-day history all came from either Pakistan (Wasim and Waqar Younis), India (Anil Kumble and Javagal Srinath) or Sri Lanka (Muttiah Muralitharan and Chaminda Vaas). So did the top six run-scorers: Sachin Tendulkar (India), Inzamam-ul-Haq (Pakistan), Sanath Jayasuriya (Sri Lanka), Sourav Ganguly, Mohammad Azharuddin (both India), and Aravinda de Silva (Sri Lanka). The subcontinent's love affair boiled down to one thing: money. And they went to great lengths to ensure a large slice of an increasingly inflated pie.

If one place summed up the new brand of cram-it-in cricket, it was Sharjah, a Gulf state which in 1971 became part of the oil-rich United Arab Emirates and proved an attractive place of work for Indian expats. Abdulrahman Bukhatir, an Arab businessman who had fallen in love with cricket during his student days in Pakistan, raised £2m to build a cricket stadium in the desert just outside Sharjah's capital city, and began staging games there in 1981. Perhaps wary of having another Packer on their hands, the national cricket boards of Australia, England, India and Pakistan selected their first official teams to contest the Rothmans Trophy there in March 1985. Live TV coverage was screened in neighbouring Dubai, and highlights were beamed to the cricket-hungry masses in India and Pakistan, whose delight at seeing Imran Khan take six for 14 to skittle India for 125 in the first game lasted only as long as it took Pakistan to be bowled out for 87. Neutral umpires added to the sense of innovation, and funds were split between profit and handouts to big-name players, along similar lines to county cricket's benefit system. Pakistan became annual visitors, and India's pilgrimages were almost as regular. Sponsorship changed virtually every year,

RIGHT Merv Hughes has the Melbourne crowd eating out of the palm of his hand during the B&H World Series final against West Indies. Hughes removed both West Indian openers to pave the way for a two-run win. January 1989

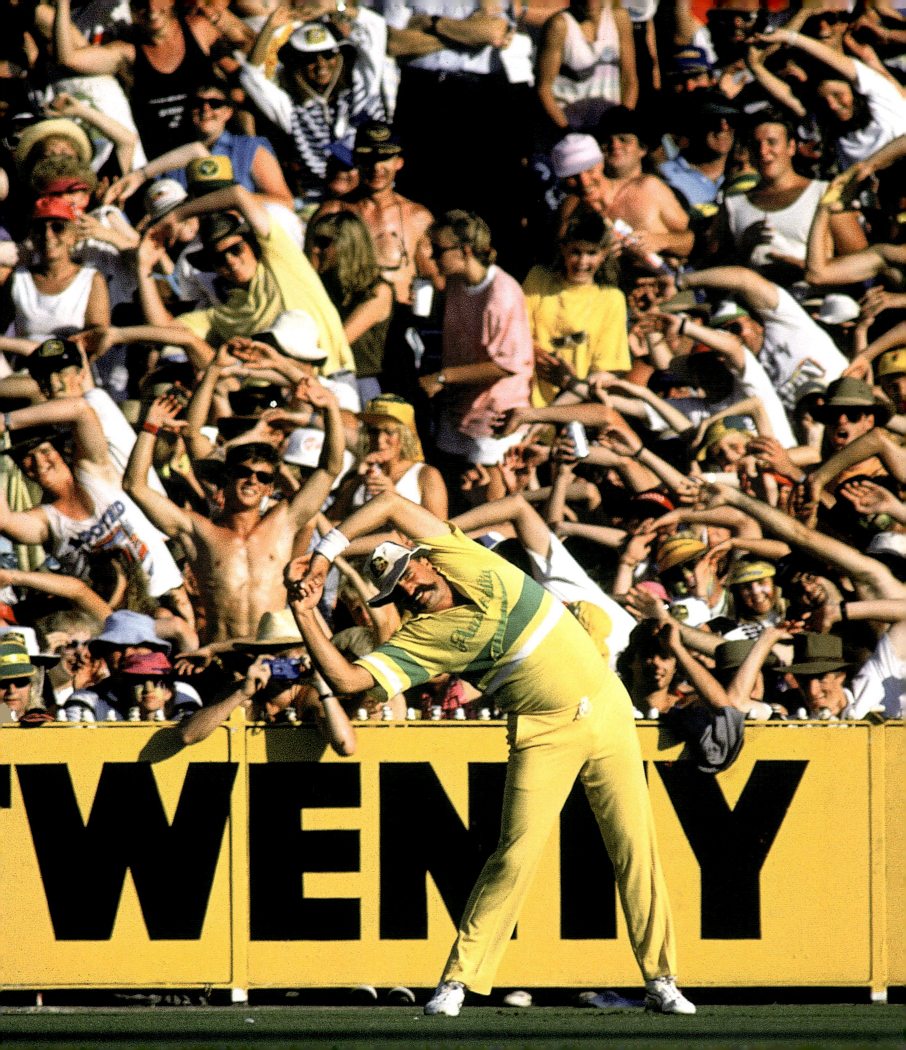

The England captain Nasser Hussain gestures angrily to the media centre after completing his one and only one-day international century against India at Lord's in the final of The NatWest Series. Several commentators had questioned his right to bat at No3.
July 2002

Following the commercial bonanza of the 1996 World Cup, when India and Pakistan churned out a profit of almost $50m between them, the subcontinent developed an even more acute awareness of the one-day game's financial possibilities. In September 1996, the two countries contested the inaugural Sahara Cup ... at the Toronto Cricket, Skating & Curling Club in Canada. The idea was not so much to spread the gospel to a landmass of cricket heathens as to attract a large satellite TV audience back in India, where pictures were beamed in from Singapore. The Sahara Cup lasted three years, and is best remembered for Inzamam-ul-Haq's bat-assisted assault on a spectator who had been taunting him through a megaphone with cries of "aloo" (Hindi for potato). Inzamam was suspended for two matches, which at least allowed him to sit out the rest of a series that was of curiosity value only.

And that was the big problem. When teams with relatively small followings, like New Zealand, Sri Lanka and Zimbabwe, gathered in some far-flung outpost to take part in the latest Champions Cup, or some other such misnomer, the temptation was to shrug and say: so what? Critics began to dismiss certain one-day internationals as meaningless, one of the adjectives sport fears most. And they used the one-day game as a convenient excuse for technical failings in the longer form of the game. As early as 1993, the *Wisden* editor Matthew Engel was writing: "It distorts cricket's skills and produces a mutant game which, while it might on occasion be tense, is essentially shallow." Set against that were the arguments outlined by Don Bradman in *Wisden* three years later. "It rids the game of the unutterable bore who thinks occupancy of the crease and his own personal aggrandisement are all that matter," he wrote, before going on to acknowledge the improvement in fielding and running between the wickets which the one-day game had helped to bring about.

But as long as the calendar contained so many days of international cricket, the opportunity for corruption was ever-present. Whispers began to circulate about the legitimacy of certain results, usually in so-called dead matches, where the outcome did not matter (Pakistan's defeat to Bangladesh in the 1999 World Cup, a result that helped Bangladesh achieve Test status, came under plenty of scrutiny). Vast sums were bet on one-day games, especially in Dubai and Indian cities like Mumbai, where gambling is illegal, and when the Cronje scandal broke in April 2000, many people's worst fears were confirmed. Ostensibly to raise money for the poorer parts of the cricket community, but perhaps motivated in part by the desire to formalise the one-day game and limit the number of meaningless matches, the ICC came up with a new tournament in October 1998, dubbed the Mini World Cup.

but with TV coverage being lapped up it was no surprise that competition to get hold of the all-important advertising slots was nearly as fierce as the cricket. It is to the venue's ever-lasting gratitude that Javed Mianded conjured up one of the great finishes of all-time in the final of the Austral-Asia Cup in April 1986. Pakistan needed four runs off the last ball to beat India, but Javed – a player who mixed street-fighting nous with a delicious sense of theatre – went even better and hit Chetan Sharma for six to take his side to a one-wicket win. Mention that game in any bar in Mumbai, Delhi or Kolkata, and you are still guaranteed a wistful shake of the head from the locals.

Held every two years, it was the only competition outside the World Cup proper to feature all the major teams, although England's lukewarm relationship with the one-day game was typified by the under-strength squad they sent to Bangladesh for the inaugural competition. That was won by South Africa, but the £10m raised for the game's development was more to the point. In 2000–1 the competition moved to Kenya, where it was known as the ICC Knockout and won by New Zealand, who lifted their first major trophy thanks to a typically rumbustious 102 not out by Chris Cairns in the final against India. But the infrastructure in both Bangladesh and Kenya had struggled to cope with the influx of the cricket world, and the 2002–3 ICC Champions Trophy – another change of name – was moved to Sri Lanka, where Colombo's monsoon season meant that the two finalists, Sri Lanka and India, had to share the spoils. In September 2004, amid mutterings that the tournament minnows were devaluing the game, Brian Lara's beleaguered West Indies stunned an England side who had spent the year thrashing them in Test matches, by recovering from 147 for eight to chase down their target of 218 in the Oval darkness.

That result meant England remained the only major nation never to have won a global competition. Many felt they had got their just deserts. For years, their attitude to the one-day game seemed to be that it was a necessary evil, a distraction from the serious stuff of Test matches. Until Emirates sponsored a three-way tournament in 1998, involving England, South Africa and Sri Lanka, the English summer had, uniquely, contained more Tests than one-day internationals. The triangular NatWest Series took over in 2000, with England beating Zimbabwe in the final, and the two-team, three-match NatWest Challenge was added in 2003, by which time England's players were starting to notch up the caps at a comparable rate to the Pakistanis, Indians and Australians. But years of neglect had taken their toll, and at successive World Cups in 1996, 1999 and 2003, England failed to cross the first significant hurdle. The rest of the world had caught up long ago.

It need not have been thus. England had been the best side for most of the 1992 World Cup, before losing out to Imran Khan's cornered tigers from Pakistan in the final. But as the 1990s wore on – and before Australia left the rest of the world for dead by winning a phenomenal 21 one-day internationals in a row in the early part of 2003 – the most consistent one-day cricket was played by South Africa. Their natural

I miss, you hit: Carlton Baugh of West Indies is indisputably bowled by Australia's Glenn McGrath during the first ODI at Sabina Park. May 2003

discipline was embodied by their captain Hansie Cronje – when he wasn't busy skulking in dark corners with bookmakers – and supplemented with flair from the likes of Jonty Rhodes, whose cover-point fielding achieved cult-status, the arch-hitter Lance Klusener and Allan Donald, for many years the fastest white bowler in the world. Between January 1996 and March 1997, South Africa won an astonishing 32 out of 36 completed games. Two of those defeats, however, explained why they also established a reputation as chokers: one came in the quarter-finals of the 1996 World Cup against West Indies, the other in the final of the Titan Cup at Mumbai against India. It was a reputation that never quite disappeared, and Australia in particular loved to remind them of it.

Despite that victory, India would soon develop a problem with big games themselves. Beginning with their defeat to Pakistan in the Pepsi Cup at Bangalore in April 1999, India lost 13 one-day finals out of 14, a sequence broken only by a stunning victory over England at Lord's in The NatWest Series in 2002. On that occasion, England reached 325 for six thanks to centuries from Marcus Trescothick and Nasser Hussain. India then slipped to 146 for five, only for Yuvraj Singh, 20, and Mohammad Kaif, 21, to add 121 and set up a dramatic two-wicket win with three balls to spare.

Anthony McGrath, the archetypal bits-and-pieces one-day cricketer, appeals against South Africa at Edgbaston. July 2003

Those games demonstrated that even within its self-imposed limits, one-day cricket at its very best could ebb and flow like a mini-Test match; and that tactics, far from being necessarily one-dimensional, could actually determine a game's outcome.

Typically, it was Australia – the country that gave the world day/night cricket and, in Melbourne in 2000, indoor one-day international cricket – who boasted two of the players responsible for revolution. For Dean Jones, running between the wickets was not so much an irritation as an art form. Ones became twos, and twos became threes as the pressure – and the sweaty palms – shifted to the fielding side. If the opposition could get rid of Jones, they had a chance. If they failed, Australia usually won: Jones was not out on 25 occasions in one-day internationals, and finished on the winning side in 20 of them. He was the first batsman to be awarded the prestigious tag of "finisher", the one-day game's highest accolade. Then came Michael Bevan, who picked up Jones's baton – Bevan's first one-day international came just eight days after Jones's last – and hared off into the distance. At Test level, Bevan never came to terms with the short-pitched delivery and averaged less than 30 in 18 games, but put him in pyjamas and he was the somnambulist supreme. His method was intuitive and yet highly scientific: he knew his own game, which meant he rarely tried to hit a boundary with a stroke he was not comfortable with, but he also adapted it to the needs of the team. His rule of thumb was that only if the required run-rate rose above seven did he feel the need to take risks, and even then the term "risk" was a relative one. In 196 one-day innings for Australia, Bevan finished not out 66 times; of those, Australia lost only 14. His average of 53.58 was in its own way as mind-boggling as Don Bradman's Test average of 99.94.

Yet neither Jones nor Bevan came even close to mixing it with one-day cricket's quickest scorers. Preferring brain to brawn, Jones scored at a rate of 72 runs per 100 balls and Bevan at 74 – miles behind Shahid Afridi of Pakistan, whose strike-rate of 102 makes him the most explosive of any player to have scored over 1000 one-day runs. And regular detonations from the likes of Ricardo Powell, Virender Sehwag, Adam Gilchrist, Andrew Symonds and Andrew Flintoff mean that one-day cricket has rarely been better served by big-hitters.

Bowlers like to moan that the one-day game is not just batsmen-friendly but bowler-hostile, and they have often had a point. But necessity has proved the mother of all kinds of inventions. Franklyn Stephenson would have played international cricket had he not been born in Barbados and played at a time when West Indies had more fast bowlers than they knew what to do with. Instead, he spent his domestic career, most notably at Nottinghamshire and Sussex, honing the finest slower yorker in the game. It was a delivery borne out of the need to keep one-day batsmen guessing, and would often crash into the base of the stumps after the batsman had guessed wrongly. Others copied him. Darren Gough, whose lack of height forced him to experiment, bowled clever off-breaks, and Adam Hollioake developed a baseball-style knuckle ball that usually elicited three different strokes from the batsman before it had even reached him. Wasim Akram and Courtney Walsh both mixed it up too, but Stephenson's most worthy successor turned out to be the Australian all-rounder Ian Harvey, a bundle of energy known by his team-mates as "Freak", who could be relied upon to bowl the pressure-ridden death overs at the end of an innings.

The slower ball was generally used as a surprise tactic, but the New Zealanders built an entire philosophy around it. Their policy of all-out defence reached its peak during the 1992 World Cup, when the trio of Gavin Larsen, Chris Harris and Rod Latham earned the collective nickname of Dibbly, Dobbly and Wobbly by taking the pace off the ball and boring the batsmen into a rash stroke. No one was quite sure who was Dibbly, who was Dobbly and who was Wobbly, but it didn't matter, and New Zealand came within a brutal innings from Inzamam-ul-Haq of reaching the final. Larsen's career economy-rate of 3.76 made him one of the meanest bowlers in the history of one-day cricket and set the benchmark for slow-medium seam-up everywhere.

But with the exception of Bevan and Larsen, the best players in one-day cricket also excelled at Test level. Sachin Tendulkar's reputation as the best batsman in the world is reinforced by the statistics he has notched up during 15 years at the crease: until the end of last September's Champions Trophy, Tendulkar had scored 13,415 runs – over 3,000 more than his nearest rival, Inzamam – and hit 37 centuries, 15 more than the next best, Sourav Ganguly. The icing on the cake was a strike-rate of 86 runs per 100 balls. Tendulkar's numerous commercial endorsements were a reminder that one-day success and monetary gain were rarely separated by more than a six-hit. Viv Richards played in financially less savvy times, but destroying an attack came just as naturally. His unbeaten 189 off 170 balls against England at Old Trafford in 1984, when he added 106 for the last wicket with Michael Holding, was a masterpiece in cold-blooded murder. But it was left to Pakistan's Saeed Anwar to outdo Richards with a swashbuckling 194 from just 146 balls against India at Chennai in May 1997 – the closest anyone had come to hitting a one-day international double-century.

Yes, one-day cricket has never quite lost its capacity to generate passion as well as cash. England fans

remember Allan Lamb hitting 18 off Bruce Reid's final over to win a World Series game at Sydney in 1986-7. Sri Lankans recall their side chasing over 300 to beat England by one wicket in a testosterone-charged game at Adelaide after Muttiah Muralitharan had been called for throwing. New Zealanders chortle at the memory of knocking Australia out of their own VB Series in 2001-2 by manipulating the bonus-points system. Pakistan reminisce about that Javed six and India wallow in that win at Lord's. West Indies have Viv. Australia have three World Cup wins and South Africa three World Cup disasters. Even Kenya and Bangladesh have pulled off high-profile shocks. One-day cricket might never move the soul in the way a Test match can, but it has made the news all the same. Whisper it, but Kerry Packer knew what he was doing.

Sanath Jayasuriya is off his feet as he cuts during Sri Lanka's four-wicket defeat by India during The NatWest Series. June 2002

Makhaya Ntini
celebrates as
Mohammad Rafique
looks back, and
Bangladesh are on their
way to defeat against
South Africa in the ICC
Champions Trophy
at Edgbaston.
September 2004

New Zealand's James
Franklin takes off after
picking up his fifth
wicket in the victory
over England at
Chester-le-Street.
July 2004

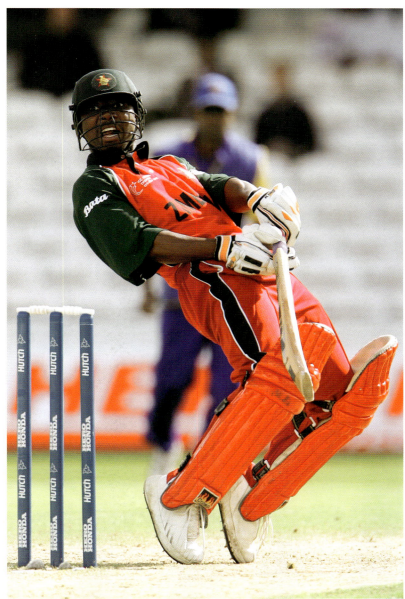

Zimbabwe captain
Tatenda Taibu takes
evasive action against
Sri Lanka at The Oval.
September 2004

LEFT White ball, white facepaint: Darren Gough prepares for battle during the ill-tempered Carlton & United Series match with Sri Lanka at Adelaide. January 1999

White Lightning: Allan Donald momentarily dispenses with the trademark glare as South Africa take on Zimbabwe at Harare. October 1995

England are in shock after turning near-certain victory into defeat in the final of The NatWest Series against India. Michael Vaughan (left), Nick Knight (centre) and Ashley Giles can't quite believe it.
July 2002

Shaun Pollock is left in no doubt about how many runs he has scored during South Africa's four-wicket defeat to England in The NatWest Series. July 2003

Nick Knight dives for safety as Ajay Ratra (right) and Harbhajan Singh hope for a run-out during the fourth ODI between India and England at Kanpur. India win the match, but the series finishes 3–3. January 2002

Mark Boucher goes
head over heels as he
attempts to run out Alec
Stewart at Old Trafford.
May 1998

Pakistan fans flood
Edgbaston following
their side's 108-run
victory over England in
The NatWest Series.
June 2001

The sun sets in the desert as fans watch a Pakistan net session ahead of their Sharjah Cup game with England.
April 1987

It's carnage at The Oval, where Yashpal Sharma (left), Syed Kirmani and David Gower (obscured) collide during England's 114-run victory over India. June 1982

Steve Waugh throws
everything into a cut
shot during Australia's
tie with England at
Trent Bridge.
May 1989

Sachin Tendulkar
gets in some catching
practice ahead of India's
clash with Pakistan
in Colombo.
July 2004

Andrew Flintoff looks
on during an England
nets session at the
County Ground
in Bristol.
July 2003

England's innings is very much a work in progress as Shane Warne bowls to Nick Knight at Melbourne. December 2002

Sun-kissed Pakistan
fans look on anxiously
as their side goes down
to arch-rivals India
at Karachi.
March 2004

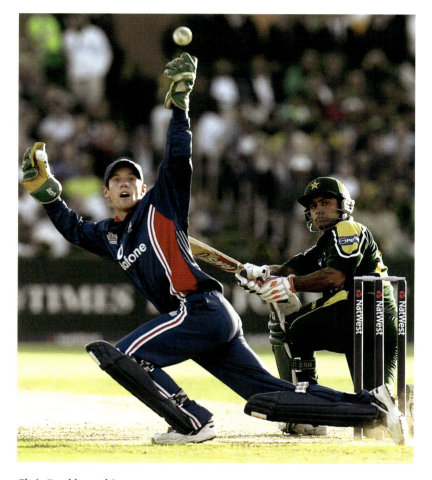

Chris Read keeps his
eye on the ball as
Pakistan's Mohammed
Hafeez rides his luck
during The NatWest
Challenge.
June 2003

RIGHT A crooked
middle stump tells the
tale as England's Gareth
Batty is bowled first ball
by Australia's Brett Lee
in a VB Series match
at Sydney.
December 2003

David Gower and Mike Gatting indulge in a half-hearted aerobics session during a one-day international between India and England.
January 1985

Reality dawns on Greg Blewett, who is bowled by Darren Gough during Australia's six-wicket defeat to England in the first Texaco Trophy match at Headingley.
May 1997

Mohammad Kaif's joyful leap confirms an astonishing Indian win in the final of the 2002 NatWest Series against England at Lord's. Set 326, India scraped home by two wickets. July 2002

Graeme Hick sees the light during a brilliant, but futile, 109 against Australia at Adelaide. January 1999

Nasser Hussain
practises his signature
as England prepare
to take on India at
Eden Gardens.
January 2002

Clive Rice takes
a breather at Eden
Gardens in Calcutta on
the eve of South Africa's
first game back
following the apartheid
years. They lost to India
by three wickets, but the
result hardly mattered.
November 1991

The covers at the
R. Premadasa Stadium
in Colombo are merely
cosmetic as the final of
the ICC Champions
Trophy is washed out.
Sri Lanka and India
share the spoils.
September 2002

The sun has set but the short sleeves are on at a packed Sydney Cricket Ground for Australia's clash with England. January 1983

Stephen Fleming looks
worried after trying to
cut Jason Gillespie
during Australia's
thrashing of New
Zealand in the ICC
Champions Trophy
at The Oval.
September 2004

Sachin Tendulkar
prepares to paddle to leg
while Alec Stewart waits
expectantly behind the
stumps in a NatWest
Series match at The Oval.
July 2002

England's James Kirtley takes one of the great Lord's catches to dismiss India's Sourav Ganguly in The NatWest Series. June 2002.

Is it a bird? Is it a plane? Or has Kaushal Lokuarachchi of Sri Lanka just dropped Australia's Andrew Symonds in Colombo? February 2004

Nail biter:
Pakistan captain
Inzamam-ul-Haq waits
his turn to bat during
the third ODI against
India in Peshawar. His
side squeezed home by
four wickets.
March 2004

The background is dramatic, though the game is anything but as India cruise to an eight-wicket win over England in the ICC Champions Trophy at the R. Premadasa Stadium in Colombo. September 2002

India's captain Sourav Ganguly celebrates the fall of an England wicket in The NatWest Challenge match at Lord's. September 2004

LEFT Darren Gough offers Pakistan opener Imran Nazir some technical advice at Old Trafford. June 2003

Jonty Rhodes clings on
by his fingertips to get
rid of Robert Croft in
an Emirates Trophy
match at Edgbaston.
August 1998

Fans are determined
that rain won't stop play
at the Queen's Park
Oval in Port-of-Spain.
April 2004

Chapter Five

The World Cup

Forty-five years after the birth of its football equivalent, but 12 years before rugby cottoned on, cricket staged its first truly global contest. The year was 1975, the World Cup something of a curiosity. The impracticalities of staging a Test championship meant the limited-overs game was the only viable format, yet just 18 one-day internationals had been staged worldwide when England met India for the tournament opener at Lord's. Naivety, it turned out, was not the preserve of the crowd alone. Replying to England's 334 for four from 60 overs, India crawled to 132 for three, with their opener Sunil Gavaskar still there at the end on 36 from 174 balls. He explained that India had no chance of getting the runs, so he had opted for batting practice, but the spectator who dumped his lunch at Gavaskar's feet in protest was not amused.

In the post-Cronje era, Gavaskar's go-slow might have attracted the interest of the ICC's Anti-Corruption Unit. In 1975 it merely looked like a horrible misjudgement. Those were innocent days, when even the players themselves seemed unsure of the merits of the competition. Since then, its growth has mirrored the development of the game itself, and by 1996, the World Cup meant big business – not just in the eyes of the cricketers, but also for the administrators, the marketing men, the spectators and the vast TV audiences, especially on the subcontinent, which could justifiably lay claim to being the game's new commercial centre, and possibly even its spiritual centre too.

In 1975, eight teams played a leisurely total of 15 matches in 15 days. In 2003, 14 teams played 54 in 43. Prize money and profits rose exponentially. Tactics evolved. Laws changed. Most cricket followers still regarded the Test match as the game's highest form, but the World Cup had made the journey from a boy-scout jamboree held only in England to a high-powered, and at times highly politicised, business convention staged all over the cricketing globe. The game changed too, reflecting its own development in the downtime between competitions. Fielding circles came into play in 1983. Neutral umpires stood for the first time in 1987. Coloured clothing with players' names was introduced in 1992. The third umpire studied his first TV monitor in 1996. The controversial Super Sixes were born in 1999. And in 2003, the number of non-Test teams rose to four.

But if evolution was an ongoing process, there were times when revolution never seemed far away. In 1996, Australia and West Indies withdrew from their matches in the Sri Lankan capital Colombo, where a terrorist bomb had injured hundreds just a few weeks earlier. Seven years later, England and New Zealand jeopardised their own participation by pulling out of matches in, respectively, Zimbabwe and Kenya on security grounds. The outside world was intruding on the game as never before; only those who preferred to bury their heads in the sand could now argue that sport and politics did not mix. During the 2003 World Cup in Africa they did not merely mix, but jostled conspicuously for position.

Following their success in the first two competitions, West Indies arrived in England in 1983 confident of emulating the feat of Brazil's footballers 13 years earlier, when they became the first side to win the Jules Rimet trophy three times. Like Brazil, West Indies were not simply the best team around – they were the most attractive too, and had been since the

1975 *Lord's*
West Indies 291/8
Australia 274
West Indies won by 17 runs

1979 *Lord's*
West Indies 286/9
England 194
West Indies won by 92 runs

1983 *Lord's*
India 183
West Indies 140
India won by 43 runs

1987–8 *Kolkata*
Australia 253/5
England 246/8
Australia won by 7 runs

1991–2 *Melbourne*
Pakistan 249/6
England 227
Pakistan won by 22 runs

1995–6 *Lahore*
Australia 241/7
Sri Lanka 245/3
Sri Lanka won by 7 wkts

1999 *Lord's*
Pakistan 132
Australia 133/2
Australia won by 8 wkts

2002–3 *Johannesburg*
Australia 359/2
India 234
Australia won by 125 runs

See pp. 308–9 for full scorecards 1980–2004

LEFT The Australian captain Ricky Ponting sinks to his knees after Darren Lehmann holds onto Zaheer Khan's miscue at mid-on to secure a 125-run victory over India in the final of the World Cup at Johannesburg. March 2003

RIGHT The India captain Kapil Dev just can't stop smiling after helping his side pull off one of the biggest shocks in World Cup history by beating West Indies in the final at Lord's. The man of the match, Mohinder Amarnath, is on the left. June 1983

inception of the competition eight years earlier. Australia had been brushed aside in the 1975 final by a combination of Clive Lloyd's brutal century and Viv Richards's aquiline fielding. And England had succumbed in 1979 thanks to the muscular batting of Richards and Collis King and the laser-like accuracy of the giant Joel Garner's bowling. Who would be the fall guys this time? The answer was a complete shock: it would be West Indies themselves.

The warning signs were there from the very start. In their opening game, West Indies lost to India by 34 runs, their first defeat in World Cup history. They recovered well, winning their five remaining group matches. But their aura of invincibility had been punctured. India's win was not the only surprise. The World Cup debutants Zimbabwe squeezed out Australia by 13 runs, with the future England coach Duncan Fletcher winning the man of the match award for an unbeaten 69 and four top-order wickets. Later, Zimbabwe would reduce India to 17 for five, only to be denied a second upset by Kapil Dev's murderous 175 not out from 138 balls in Tunbridge Wells, where for once onlookers were not so much disgusted as disbelieving.

India duly qualified for the last four, where they saw off England with ease, but in the other semi-final West Indies were grateful for a curious Gavaskar-like innings by the Pakistan opener Mohsin Khan, who made 70 off 176 balls to set up a match-losing total of 184. The final was expected to be just as one-sided,

and when India, 66–1 also-rans at the start of the tournament, subsided to 183 all out, cricket writers everywhere began to pen their hymns of praise to one of sport's greatest teams. Instead, West Indies were bundled out for 143 by the hittable medium-pace of Madan Lal (3–31) and Mohinder Amarnath (3–12). India were rewarded with a cheque for £20,000, a figure that had ballooned to $2m (£1.27m) when Australia lifted the trophy in 2003. In fact, even a solitary victory in a Super Six match in 2003 brought as much as £25,000. But the pulling power of the World Cup was only just beginning.

In late 1987, the competition moved away from England for the first time and headed east to the subcontinent. Matches were reduced from 60 overs-a-side to 50 because of the shorter daylight hours in Pakistan and India. Meanwhile, the presence of neutral umpires for the first time meant that any whingeing about decisions could no longer contain the charge of bias. The participants were the same as in 1983 (the seven eligible Test sides – South Africa were still banned – plus Zimbabwe), but the expectations were very different. Where the previous World Cups had been dominated by seamers, the drier pitches of south Asia would benefit the spinners – and that, in effect, meant the hosts. The clamour for an all-Asian final gave the competition an edge it had previously lacked. Stiff-upper-lip applause in the Lord's pavilion was one thing; several thousand delirious Indians or Pakistanis, pulsating like the game's jugular itself, was quite another.

They were going according to plan when India and Pakistan glided into the last four, but then things started to unravel. Pakistan faced Australia at Lahore and appeared to be on top before Steve Waugh took 18 runs off the last over of the innings to set 268. At 150 for three, Pakistan were again on course for the final, only for Craig McDermott to trip them up with five for 44. If that was hard for the locals to stomach, worse was to follow at Bombay. The England opener Graham Gooch had spent the previous day in the nets driving the local spinners to distraction by sweeping anything and everything, and now he put his plan into practice against India's two slow left-armers, Maninder Singh and Ravi Shastri. Gooch's 115 helped England to a match-winning 254 for six, and the subcontinental party had been well and truly gatecrashed. But if the organisers couldn't have an India–Pakistan final, they got the next best thing: England v Australia.

It was a game that would be defined by a single shot. England had reached 135 for two in pursuit of Australia's 253 for five when the Australian captain Allan Border decided to try out his own occasional left-arm tweakers. His opposite number Mike Gatting,

Australia's Dean Jones (left) and Craig McDermott provide their captain Allan Border with a shoulder to lean on after beating England in the World Cup final at Calcutta. November 1987

WESSELS
HUDSON
KIRSTEN
KUIPER
CRONJE
RHODES
MCMILLAN
RICH'SON
SNELL
PRINGLE
DONALD
RUSHMERE

SOUTH AFRICA
TO WIN
NEED 22 RUNS
OFF 1 BALL

10:08

MITSUBISHI ELECTRIC

GOOCH
BOTHAM
STEWART
HICK
FAIR'HER
LAMB
LEWIS
REEVE
DEFR'TAS
IL'WORTH
SMALL
TUFNELL

YABBA'S HILL

Ansett Australia.   Budget   Benson & Hedges Wor

well set on 41, tried to reverse-sweep his first delivery but succeeded only in lobbing a gentle catch to the wicket-keeper Greg Dyer. England eventually fell eight runs short.

In 1975 and 1979 the tournament had contained 15 matches; in 1983 and 1987 the figure had risen to 27. Now, in 1992, it reached 39, with Australia staging 25 and New Zealand 14. There was a new sponsor – Benson and Hedges – and a new format. Instead of two groups of four, with each side playing the others twice to determine the semi-finalists, there was a league of nine – including, for the first time, South Africa – in which everyone played everyone else once, with the top four teams progressing. One critic called the new system "as exciting as the Nullarbor Plain", but most were agreed it was the fairest yet. In came coloured clothing, floodlights and a white ball – or, to be precise, two white balls: one at either end to prevent them from becoming too discoloured, a move which delighted the swing-bowlers' union. But the most revolutionary change concerned the fielding circle. In previous World Cups, four fielders were obliged to remain within the circle throughout the innings. Now, in an attempt to inject some life into the early stages of an innings, only two fielders were allowed outside the circle during the first 15 overs, thus leaving inviting gaps in the outfield for the top-order batsmen to exploit.

The law-change even spawned a new entry in cricket's lexicon: the pinch-hitter. Until now, the term had been confined to baseball, where it denotes a substitute player brought in specifically for his batting. Cricket subtly subverted the definition, using it to describe a batsman, often promoted up the order, who went for his shots from the start. The term really gained currency at the 1996 World Cup, when Sri Lanka's openers briefly went ballistic. But cricket's first pinch-hitter was New Zealand's bewhiskered Mark Greatbatch, who lit up the group stages of the 1992 competition with a series of clumps that left bowlers dazed and the crowds scattering for cover. In seven matches he plundered 313 runs off 356 balls, hitting 32 fours and 13 sixes and taking New Zealand to the brink of their first final.

New Zealand had dominated the early stages of the competition, winning their first seven group matches and scoring points for lateral thinking: the off-spinner Dipak Patel opened the bowling in all but two of his nine games and went for just 3.10 runs an over. England, though, were not far behind. The

Farce at Sydney, where the rain rules leave South Africa with an impossible task in their semi-final against England. March 1992

Sri Lanka's captain Arjuna Ranatunga steers to third man on his way to 47 not out off only 37 balls to help his side beat Australia in the final at Lahore. March 1996

Kenya's Kennedy Otieno and the Australian wicketkeeper Ian Healy play spot the ball during a group game at Visakhapatnam. Otieno hits 85 but Australia ease home by 97 runs. February 1996

highlight of their opening sequence of five wins from six came when Ian Botham roused himself for one last bout of Aussie-bashing, with a spell of four wickets for no runs in seven balls and a meaty half-century. And it would have been six wins out of six but for the rain at Adelaide, where England had bowled out Pakistan for 74, only to be limited to 24 for one by the weather. Had Pakistan lost, the chances are they would not have made it through to the semi-finals. But a rallying cry from their 39-year-old captain Imran Khan rebounded off the walls of the Pakistan dressing-room and straight into cricket folklore. He told his team to fight like cornered tigers; they responded by roaring to victory in their final three group games to squeeze into the last four ahead of Australia and West Indies. They were joined by New Zealand, England and South Africa.

Both semi-finals linger in the memory, but for different reasons. At Auckland, the home crowd broke into a chorus of "We're in the final" as Pakistan fell hopelessly behind the run-rate in pursuit of New Zealand's 262 for seven, but they were soon silenced by a bullocking innings from the 22-year-old Inzamam-ul-Haq, who blasted 60 from 37 balls to turn the game on its head. The following day at Sydney, Kiwi disappointment made way for South African despair. Set 252 in 43 overs, South Africa required 22 off 13 balls with four wickets left. Then the heavens opened, activating the competition's absurd rain rules, which had been drawn up to accommodate TV schedules rather than the good of the game. Two overs were lost, but rather than recalculate the required run-rate, the South Africans' target was reduced by subtracting the two most economical overs in the England innings: in this case a pair of Meyrick Pringle maidens. Brian McMillan was now left with the impossible task of scoring 22 runs off one delivery, and patted a forlorn single. One of the most important games in World Cup history had ended in farce.

Gooch's England, though, were not complaining. Despite fading after a heady start, they now found themselves in their third World Cup final out of five. In front of an MCG crowd of 87,182, most of them baying for Pommie blood, England's prospects looked good when Derek Pringle removed both Pakistan openers cheaply. But Javed Miandad, Imran Khan and more fireworks from Inzamam helped Pakistan to 249 for six, and when Wasim Akram removed Botham for a duck and Graeme Hick fell for Mushtaq Ahmed's googly, England were up against it. Neil Fairbrother and Allan Lamb gave them some hope, but Wasim returned to dismiss Lamb and Chris Lewis in successive deliveries – both of them unplayable – and Pakistan went on to clinch their first World Cup. Imran dedicated the win to a cancer hospital in Lahore, and called it "the most fulfilling and satisfying cricket moment of my life". A typically down-at-heel Gooch, who had played in all three of England's losing finals, remarked: "It's not the end of the world, but it is close to it."

If the commercially influenced South Africa-England semi-final had been a wake-up call to the game, then the 1996 Wills World Cup, staged jointly by India, Pakistan and – for the first time – Sri Lanka, was one long ear-splitting siren. Alarm bells began to ring as early as the opening ceremony in Calcutta, where a series of embarrassing technical malfunctions were a sign of things to come: there was too much travel, too many meaningless matches – 30 in all – to determine eight predictable quarter-finalists, and poor practice facilities. As the former cricket correspondent of *The Times*, Alan Lee, put it in the *Wisden Almanack*: "The impression was that the cricket was secondary to the commercialism". A general atmosphere of chaos was not helped when Australia and West Indies both pulled out of their group games in Colombo because of concerns about terrorism. And for the first time in World Cup history a match had to be abandoned because of crowd trouble, when a group of Indian fans in Calcutta could not accept the fact that their team was about to lose their semi-final against Sri Lanka, and decided to throw bottles onto the pitch and start fires in the stands. But as cricket held its head in shame off the pitch, a romantic tale had unfolded on it.

Sri Lanka were the only major Asian cricketing power not to have lifted the trophy, but their top-order explosions lit up stadiums across the subcontinent. Sanath Jayasuriya – a sort of Greatbatch-plus – led the way, brutalising a poor England side in the quarter-finals with 82 from 44 balls, and finishing the competition with a strike-rate of 132 per 100 deliveries. Sri Lanka became the team the neutrals couldn't help warming to. In the other half of the draw, West Indies emerged from the embarrassment of losing to Kenya to eliminate South Africa in the quarter-finals, thanks to a glittering 94-ball 111 from Brian Lara.

Their opponents in the last four were fellow refuseniks Australia, who surpassed New Zealand's spirited 286 for nine at Madras courtesy of a third World Cup century from Mark Waugh. Three days later at Mohali, however, Australia looked to be on their way home at 15 for four. Stuart Law and Michael Bevan lifted them to 207 for eight, but when West Indies cruised to 165 for two in reply, they were eyeing up a record fourth final. Then, panic: eight wickets went down for 37, leaving the captain Richie Richardson, playing the last of his 224 one-day internationals, speechless on 49 not out. The final would be between the hosts, Sri Lanka, and the team who had declined to play them exactly a month earlier, Australia. And there was also a strange sense of inevitability about the result. From 23 for two, Sri Lanka never looked back as they chased down Australia's panic-stricken 241 for seven with 22 balls and seven wickets in hand, to become the first side to win the World Cup batting second. The hero was Aravinda de Silva, who became the third player – after Clive Lloyd and Viv Richards – to score a hundred in a World Cup final, and shepherded Sri Lanka home with the help of his captain Arjuna Ranatunga. Underdogs the world over rejoiced.

Australia licked their wounds and prepared for 1999, when the World Cup, now organised by the ICC, returned to England for the first time in 16 years, with Wales, Scotland, Ireland and the Netherlands also hosting matches. Sponsored by NatWest, along with Vodafone, Pepsi and Emirates Airlines, the tournament was memorable for one almighty cock-up, one astonishing innings, and one never-to-be-repeated match. The cock-up belonged to the hosts, who contrived to miss out on qualification for the new Super Six stage. In an unlikely sequence of events, Zimbabwe beat South Africa, who had already made it through, before India thrashed England at Edgbaston. With three weeks still to go, the hosts were out.

Delirium for Australia, disaster for South Africa: Allan Donald is run out at Edgbaston with the scores level and Australia are through to the final, courtesy of finishing higher in the Super Six table. June 1999

Shoaib Akhtar prepares to take off after yorking the New Zealand captain Stephen Fleming for 41 in the semi-final at Old Trafford. Pakistan go on to win by nine wickets. June 1999

The pre-tournament favourites Australia had also struggled early on, and defeats to New Zealand and Pakistan left them knowing that another loss would prove fatal. But that was just how their captain, Steve Waugh, liked it. When he walked out to bat in the last of the Super Six matches, against South Africa at Headingley, Australia were 48 for three in reply to 271 for seven, only for Waugh to hit an unbeaten 120, one of the greatest one-day innings, to guide them into the semi-finals with two balls to spare. That Waugh also came up with one of cricket's best sledges was merely a bonus. On 56, he had worked Lance Klusener to midwicket, where Herschelle Gibbs held a simple catch before disastrously dropping the ball in the act of celebration. Waugh reputedly told Gibbs at the time: "You've just dropped the World Cup." If that was to prove sickeningly prophetic for the South Africans, worse was to come.

The two sides were drawn together for the second semi-final four days later at Edgbaston, with the prize of a place in the final against Pakistan, who had overwhelmed New Zealand the day before at Old Trafford, awaiting them. Australia began with a below-par 213, but a tour de force from Shane Warne kept them in the hunt. In the end, it boiled down to the final over, which South Africa began on 205 for nine. Lance Klusener, one of the stars of the competition so far, hammered Damien Fleming's first two deliveries through the off side to bring the scores level. But a tie would not be good enough for South Africa, who had finished below Australia in the Super Sixes. Two balls later, Klusener pulled towards mid-on and set off for the winning single. But the No 11 Allan Donald was waiting to see whether the ball beat the infield, and responded too late before dropping his bat. As Donald watched in horror, the Australians calmly rolled the ball to the striker's end, where Adam Gilchrist jubilantly removed the bails. "It was a moment of absolute madness," remembers Donald. "I wasn't such a popular man when I got home." South

Africa were heartbroken, Australia delirious. Inevitably, perhaps, the final against Pakistan was one big anticlimax. Pakistan were bundled out for 132 as Warne picked up four more wickets, and it was left to Darren Lehmann to cut the winning runs with almost 30 overs to spare. Forget Pakistan's cornered tigers of 1992. All hail the wounded wallabies.

Australia's reign of terror was only just beginning, and it would continue in some style nearly four years later in South Africa. But the 2003 World Cup would be remembered as much for its controversy as for the brilliance of Australia. There was a sharp intake of breath when Shane Warne was sent home without playing a game after testing positive for two banned diuretics. And there was much gritting of teeth over the tiresome issue of ambush marketing, a phenomenon whereby rivals of official competition sponsors seek to muscle in on their territory. But the most emotive issue by far was Zimbabwe. Two of their players, Andy Flower and Henry Olonga, took the field for their opening match with Namibia wearing black armbands, explaining that they were "mourning the death of democracy in our beloved country". Olonga was subsequently dropped, but when the selectors tried to do the same to Flower, his team-mates rebelled, forcing the selectors' hand.

All the while, the England team were agonising over whether or not to fulfil their fixture in Harare. Many of the players felt it was morally wrong to play a game of cricket when peaceful demonstrations against the Robert Mugabe regime were being punished by arrest and torture, and when they received a death threat from a group of activists calling themselves the Sons and Daughters of Zimbabwe, they decided enough was enough. England pulled out of the fixture for safety reasons, but the ICC were unmoved and awarded the points to Zimbabwe. It was a decision that would later cost England their place in the competition. New Zealand also missed out on easy points after refusing on security grounds to travel to Nairobi to play Kenya – a move that would ultimately cost them too.

Much of the cricket, though, was gripping. Pakistan's Shoaib Akhtar sent down cricket's first recorded 100mph delivery, even if England's Nick Knight defused the missile with ease. Canada's John Davison smashed a 67-ball century against West Indies, the fastest in World Cup history, and Kenya delighted everyone by beating Sri Lanka, Bangladesh and then Zimbabwe to reach the semi-finals. But the hard-luck story belonged, once more, to South Africa. When rain intervened during their must-win group game against Sri Lanka at Durban, the Duckworth/Lewis system deemed that the match was a tie. Only later did it

emerge that Mark Boucher, who defensively played the final ball before the game was abandoned straight to midwicket, had no idea that South Africa needed one more run. For the second successive World Cup, they had fallen a single run short of survival.

With the hosts out, only an improving Indian side stood in the way of the rampant Australians. India had won eight games in a row to reach the final at Johannesburg, ending Kenya's dreams on the way, but they fluffed their lines badly from the moment Sourav Ganguly won the toss and asked Australia to bat. They needed no second invitation, and the Australian captain Ricky Ponting helped himself to a stunning unbeaten 140 from just 121 balls, including eight sixes. Australia racked up 359 for two before India folded to 234.

Like Australia's total, the 2003 World Cup dwarfed anything that had gone before. Competition profits totalled $194m, a rise of nearly 300% from 1999. It was a far cry from 1975, when Prudential had sponsored the competition for £100,000. In 1996, sponsors were having to fork out £40,000 just to get their name on one of the advertising hoardings around the boundary. If the cricket had changed beyond measure, then its financial worth had become almost immeasurable too.

In his last game for Zimbabwe, against Sri Lanka at East London, Andy Flower stands next to 12th man Henry Olonga. In Zimbabwe's opening match in the tournament, the pair had worn black armbands to "mourn the death of democracy in our beloved country". Olonga was dropped, while Flower was only reinstated after a player revolt.
March 2003

Michael Holding (right, removing gloves) trudges off at Lord's, seemingly oblivious to the chaos around him. Holding has just been dismissed for six to give the 1983 World Cup to India. Joel Garner at least has a pair of souvenirs to take home. June 1983

TOP South Africa's Mark Boucher makes absolutely certain of running out Moin Khan of Pakistan in a Super Six match at Trent Bridge. South Africa win by three wickets. June 1999

BOTTOM The New Zealand captain Lee Germon is too quick for Mike Atherton, who is acting as a runner for Graeme Hick during England's defeat at Ahmedabad. February 1996

The stump camera gets a close-up as South Africa's Brian McMillan bowls Ian Botham at Melbourne. England fight back, however, to win by three wickets – their 11th one-day international victory in a row.
March 1992

Indian fans just can't get their heads round Sourav Ganguly's decision to bat first in the 2003 World Cup final. Australia make 359 for two, before dismissing India for 234.
March 2003

England's bowlers get to work under the cross of St George during their group game with Pakistan at Newlands in Cape Town. Jimmy Anderson's four for 29 swings England to a 112-run win.
February 2003

Imitation is not the
sincerest form of flattery:
Javed Miandad loses
patience with the
wicketkeeper Kiran
More's vociferous
appealing during
Pakistan's defeat to India.
March 1992

Wasim Akram (left) and
Javed Miandad are
brothers-in-arms after
Pakistan's victory over
England in the World
Cup final at Melbourne.
March 1992

Pakistan's Saeed Anwar takes time out during practice in South Africa. February 2003

Indian fans pray for the national team in Calcutta. Their pleas were answered with a storming run to the final – but then Australia ended their hopes.
February 2003

A Zimbabwe fan goes under cover to shelter from the rain during the crucial pool game with Pakistan at Bulawayo. The match is abandoned, taking Zimbabwe through to the Super Six stage, but eliminating both Pakistan and England.
March 2003

Brian Lara (left) and
Shivnarine
Chanderpaul look
concerned as they cross
for a single during West
Indies' game with
Bangladesh at Benoni.
Lara went on to make
46 and Chanderpaul 29
in West Indies' total of
244 for nine, but rain
had the final say.
February 2003

Aravinda de Silva (right) exchanges high-fives with Romesh Kaluwitharana after bowling Ricky Ponting for 45 in the 1996 World Cup final. De Silva later added the man of the match award for his unbeaten 107 as Sri Lanka cruised home by seven wickets. March 1996

Glenn McGrath
summons up a beauty
to bowl the West Indies
captain Brian Lara on
his way to figures of five
for 14 at Old Trafford.
Australia win by
six wickets.
May 1999

The only way is up, it
seems, for England's
Jimmy Anderson, who
celebrates a superb
yorker to get rid of
Pakistan's Yousuf
Youhana for a duck
under the lights at
Cape Town.
February 2003

The Netherlands captain Roland Lefebvre can see the funny side after ducking out of the way of an Andy Bichel bouncer at Potchefstroom. To no one's great surprise, Australia win by 75 runs. February 2003

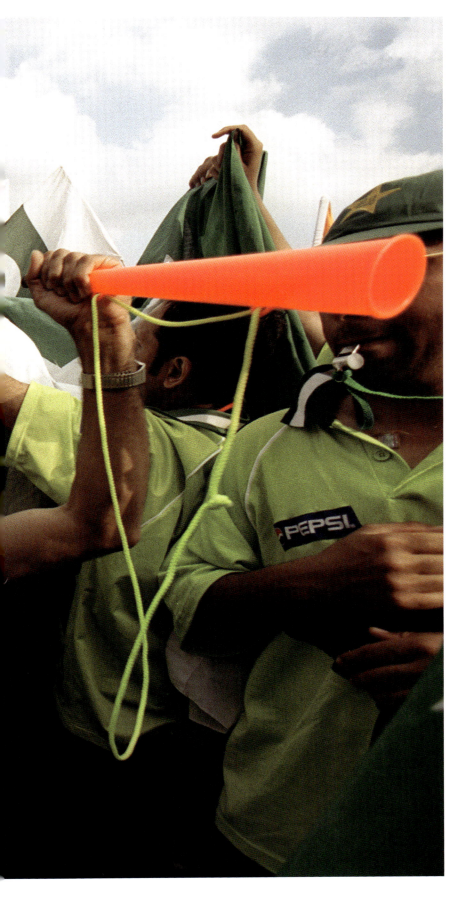

Pakistan's fans are green and proud of it at the Super Six clash with arch-rivals India at Old Trafford. India win by 47 runs, but Pakistan go on to reach the final. June 1999

The boundary count is in danger of getting out of control during the India-Pakistan quarter-final at Bangalore. India hold on to the south Asian bragging-rights with a 39-run win. March 1996

In an unusual role reversal, Jonty Rhodes hurls himself rather than the ball at the stumps. Rhodes makes his ground during South Africa's Super Six game against Australia at Headingley, but Steve Waugh's epic unbeaten 120 steers Australia home.
June 1999

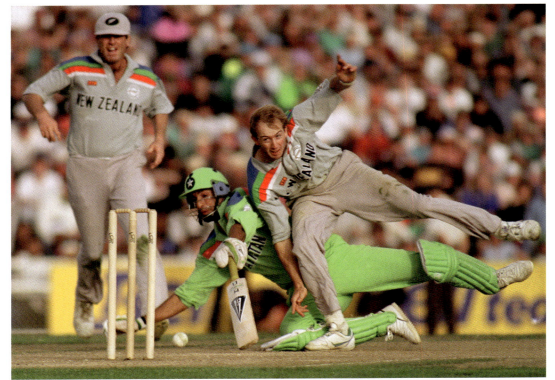

New Zealand's Chris Harris tries a novel method of running out Pakistan's Wasim Akram in the semi-final at Auckland. Wasim survives and Pakistan silence the home crowd to win by four wickets.
March 1992

LEFT He wasn't everyone's favourite cricketer, but the Sri Lanka captain Arjuna Ranatunga helped a nation stand up for itself and even win a World Cup.
May 1999

Eden Gardens in
Calcutta is packed to its
110,000 capacity for the
semi-final between
India and Sri Lanka.
The match is awarded
to Sri Lanka when
crowd trouble breaks
out with India on the
brink of defeat.
March 1996

A lathi-toting member of the riot police steps in as the Calcutta crowd vents its frustration at India's performance. March 1996

A steward is unimpressed as Dennis Lillee shows off his thighs before Australia's World Cup warm-up game with Sussex at Hove.
June 1983

Beyond the call of the duty: West Indies' Ramnaresh Sarwan returns from his hospital bed to resume his innings at Cape Town, but Sri Lanka won by six runs. February 2003

Australia's wicketkeeper Adam Gilchrist dives for a catch during the World Cup match against England at St George's Park in Port Elizabeth, South Africa. March 2003

TOP LEFT Soaking up the atmosphere: groundstaff at Rawalpindi dry out the pitch in advance of England's 78-run defeat by South Africa. February 1996

BOTTOM LEFT Michael Atherton's alter ego fails to impress as England lose against New Zealand at Ahmedabad after Nathan Astle's century. February 1996

Darren Gough is on his best behaviour after a workout with his skipping-rope at Lahore. February 1996

Chris Cairns tries to run
Shane Warne out
during New Zealand's
surprise victory over
Australia at Cardiff.
May 1999

Allan Lamb looks back anxiously during England's 1987 World Cup final defeat to Australia, a game still remembered in England for Mike Gatting's fatal reverse-sweep. November 1987

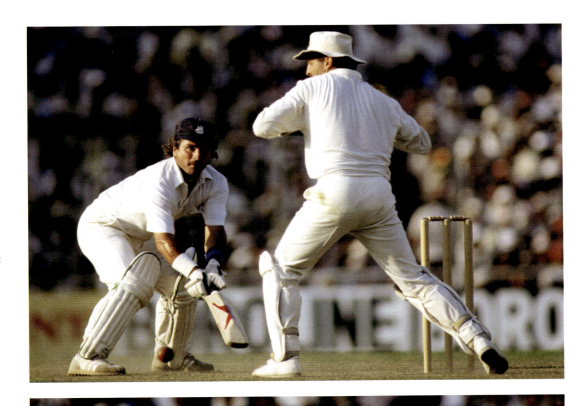

Kapil Dev gets lucky against Phil DeFreitas in the semi-final at Mumbai, but England have the last laugh, winning by 35 runs thanks to 115 from the sweep-happy Graham Gooch, and four wickets for Eddie Hemmings. November 1987

The Australian left-arm
wrist-spinner Brad Hogg
leaves members of the
media in the dark
during an invitation net
session at Grey High
School in Port Elizabeth.
February 2003

Ricky Ponting, Australia's captain, hits out in his unbeaten 140 from 121 balls during the 2003 final against India at Johannesburg. Ponting smashed eight sixes to help Australia to 359 for two and a 125-run win.
March 2003

Chapter Six

The Icons

Sachin Tendulkar has probably spent more time signing autographs than any player in history. Here he keeps his fans happy at the Melbourne Cricket Ground. December 1999

A common sporting refrain insists that no individual is bigger than the game. By definition this must be correct, but it doesn't mean that no one has had a go at disproving it. Think of Pelé, Jack Nicklaus, Pete Sampras, Michael Schumacher, Steve Redgrave and Ed Moses. And think of cricket. The last 25 years have not merely produced some of the greatest players in its history, which in any case is longer than that of most sports. They have produced players who, whether through sheer brilliance or charisma, have succeeded in elevating the game above its immediate context; who score runs, take wickets, hold catches, and yet do much more; who have set trends or defied them and usually both; and who, most importantly, have allowed spectators to lose themselves in the here and now.

Our selection of cricket's 10 greatest icons from the last 25 years was not easy, and is certainly not infallible. How, after all, do you leave out a player like Kapil Dev, who proved that fast bowlers could flourish in the subcontinent? Or Shaun Pollock, South Africa's metronome par excellence? Or Matthew Hayden, who once hit nine Test centuries in just over a year?

Or Curtly Ambrose or Adam Gilchrist or Glenn McGrath or Allan Donald? Or Ricky Ponting, Wasim Akram, Rahul Dravid, Courtney Walsh, David Gower and Waqar Younis? With a sense of foreboding, that's how.

The 10 we settled on were chosen because of the unique gifts they brought to the party, to use a favourite phrase among the captains and coaches of today. And each one has a story to tell. The pomp of Ian Botham, blowing away the Aussies. The power of Viv Richards, infusing the downtrodden Caribbean with new pride. The stealth of Richard Hadlee, fighting a lone battle to distract New Zealand from rugby. The grace of Imran Khan, daring Pakistan to bowl fast. The genius of Sachin Tendulkar, holding the hopes of a billion Indians in his hands. The wizardry of Shane Warne, reigniting the flames of leg-spin. The bedazzlement of Brian Lara, breaking records while those around him fail. The mystique of Muttiah Muralitharan, putting Sri Lanka on the world map. The grit of Steve Waugh, rewriting history with single-mindedness. And the raucousness of Andrew Flintoff, breathing new life into the nation that invented the game.

LEFT Ian Botham has just smashed Australia for 149 during the famous Headingley Test. The cigar seems well deserved. July 1981

Brian Lara

WEST INDIES

Lara reaches 300 on his way to Test cricket's first quadruple-century against England at St John's, Antigua. April 2004

There was always something of the prodigy about Brian Lara, but it was not until 1994 that the world sat bolt upright and took notice. In the space of seven heady weeks, he broke cricket's two most treasured batting records, shattering nearly 72 years of combined history in the process. First he hit a Test-record 375 for West Indies against England in Antigua. Then, with the superlatives still ringing in his ears, he became first-class cricket's first quintuple-centurion with an innings of 501 not out for Warwickshire against Durham in the county championship at Edgbaston. At the age of 25 Lara was, in the words of the Caribbean cricket broadcaster Tony Cozier, "cricket's first truly international megastar". Destiny would have had it no other way.

Football or even accountancy could have claimed him, but his father made sure that cricket did, and at 21 he made an accomplished 44 on Test debut against a Pakistan attack including Imran Khan, Wasim Akram, Waqar Younis and Abdul Qadir. Two years – but only four Tests – later, Lara hit a sumptuous 277 against Australia at Sydney, starting a love affair with big scores that turned into an addiction: average out his Test hundreds and you get almost 190.

Some patches were even purpler than others. In England in 1995, he made 641 runs in four innings; in 1999 he singlehandedly held the Australians at home; and in late 2001 he totalled 688 in three Tests in Sri Lanka, scoring 45% of his side's runs off the bat. With Caribbean cricket desperate for heroes, Lara was usually the answer, even if he occasionally behaved as if he was all too aware of the fact. But the thirst for glory remained: when he briefly lost his Test record to the Australian opener Matthew Hayden, he reclaimed it within six months thanks to a monstrous innings of 400 not out, again in Antigua, again against England. The whippy wrists, the whirring blade, the flashing grin: Lara's trademarks are as indelibly etched in the mind's eye as his runs are in the record books.

TESTS
1990–2004
Caps 112
Runs 10,094 @ 52.84
HS 400*
100s 26 **50s** 46
Capt W10 L23 D7

ONE-DAY INTERNATIONALS
1990–2004
Caps 244
Runs 8,921 @ 42.27
HS 169 **SR** 79.30
100s 18 **50s** 55
Wkts 4 @ 15.25
BB 2/5 **R/O** 7.46
Capt W36 L38 NR5

RIGHT Lara feels the heat on West Indies' troubled tour of Australia. November 2000

Some typical
flamboyance against
England at Lord's.
July 2004

Relaxing in the St John's dressing-room in Antigua, where Lara broke Garry Sobers's 36-year-old world record with an innings of 375 against England. April 1994

Ten years later, he went 25 runs better on the same ground, reclaiming his world record from Australia's Matthew Hayden with an unbeaten 400 – also against England. April 2004

Steve Waugh

AUSTRALIA

LEFT Waugh cuts a chiselled figure after yet another Ashes series triumph, this time at the WACA in Perth. December 2002

ABOVE Waugh has just driven Richard Dawson through the covers for four to reach a century off the last ball of the day in front of his home crowd at Sydney. January 2003

On August 4, 2001, Steve Waugh was stretchered off the field towards the end of the third Test against England at Trent Bridge after tearing his left calf. It was the sort of injury that would have ruled most players out for several weeks. But Waugh loved a challenge, and 19 days later he resumed the captaincy of Australia for the fifth Test at The Oval. It surprised no one when he hobbled his way to an unbeaten 157 – an innings that typified a man who in turn typified a certain type of Australian.

Waugh never knew when he was beaten, which in any case was not very often. He was a slow starter – he didn't score a Test century until his 42nd innings – but once he got going, there was no turning back. By the time he retired to a hero's farewell at his home ground in Sydney in January 2004, more than 19 years after his Test debut, he had become the most impressive cricketer of his age.

Waugh was not just about runs, although when he retired only his compatriot Allan Border stood ahead of his Test tally of 10,927. He was not just about longevity, although no one won more than his 168 caps. He was not even just about records, although no captain had ever presided over a team that won 16 Tests in a row, as Australia did between October 1999 and March 2001. Waugh was all this and more. He became, by no one's particular appointment and to the irritation of some, an unofficial worldwide spokesman for the game. He published diaries of his many tours. And he helped set up a home for daughters of leprosy victims in the village of Udayan, near Calcutta. Waugh's sense of perspective was one of his greatest gifts to the game.

He will always be remembered as a hard-as-nails competitor, a gutsy, pragmatic armadillo of a batsman and a ruthless captain who led one of the best teams in sporting history with a single-mindedness that, at times, bordered on the bullying. But he was also part of Australia's fabric, and for a brief while around his retirement, the red handkerchief he used to wear while batting became as much a part of his nation's consciousness as the kangaroo or Ayers Rock.

TESTS
1985–2004
Caps 168
Runs 10,927 @ 51.06
HS 200
100s 32 **50s** 50
Wkts 92 @ 37.44
BB 5/28 **5ws** 3
Capt W41 L9 D7

ONE-DAY INTERNATIONALS
1986–2002
Caps 325
Runs 7,569 @ 32.90
HS 120* **SR** 75.91
100s 3 **50s** 45
Wkts 195 @ 34.67
BB 4/33 **R/O** 4.56
Capt W67 L35 T3 NR1

FAR LEFT Keeping a thin-eyed watch over his troops before the playing of the national anthems at the Brisbane Test against West Indies. Australia won inside three days. November 2000

Throwing everything into a square-cut against England at Sydney. January 2003

In his last match for New South Wales, Waugh takes advantage of a rain break to satisfy another autograph hunter at Sydney. March 2004

Viv Richards

WEST INDIES

Throughout the glory years of the 1980s, West Indian intimidation was usually personified by their lethal four-man pace attack. But it was also bound up in the bat of one individual. Viv – rarely has so small a word spelled so much danger. Years before Matthew Hayden tried to bully bowlers by taking guard a foot outside his crease and biffing them over the top, Richards employed psychology of a wholly different kind, swaggering to the crease then glaring contemptuously at the bowler, as if to say "come and dismiss me if you think you're man enough".

He never batted in a helmet, preferring instead the West Indian maroon cap, which reflected his enormous pride in the region and gave a misleading impression of tidy conformity. At times, the only principle he conformed to was that of murdering the bowlers. It could be impossible to keep him quiet, especially when showing off his party piece – the whip through midwicket after the bowler thought he was about to clip the top of off stump.

If Sir Donald Bradman overwhelmed the opposition through sheer volume of runs, Richards simply frightened the pants off them. His unbeaten 189 during a one-day international against England at Old Trafford in 1984 was a spectacular masterpiece in mayhem. His 56-ball century, which remains the quickest in Test history, also against England in his home town of St John's in Antigua in April 1986, was even better.

Richards scored his runs in the day before freebies were handed out by a new Sri Lankan side, Zimbabwe and Bangladesh; 70 of his 121 Tests came against either England or Australia. And he kept going until the end, hitting five half-centuries during his farewell series in England in 1991, and scoring 60 in his last knock at The Oval when he needed 20 to retire with a Test average of 50.

Viv Richards was a visceral and inspiring leader, captaining the West Indies to 27 victories out of 50, and a panther in the field. But what was he like to bowl to? The former England paceman Bob Willis summed it up: "He hit my good balls for four and my bad ones for six." That was Viv – the first of the intimidatory batsmen.

TESTS
1974–1991
Caps 121
Runs 8,540 @ 50.23
HS 291
100s 24 **50s** 45
Wkts 32 @ 61.37
BB 2/17
Capt W27 L8 D15

ONE-DAY INTERNATIONALS
1975–1991
Caps 187
Runs 6,721 @ 47.00
HS 189* **SR** 90.20
100s 11 **50s** 45
Wkts 118 @ 35.83
BB 6/41 **R/O** 4.48
Capt W67 L36 NR2

LEFT A typically swaggering pose against Australia at Melbourne. December 1988.

Richards hooks his good mate Ian Botham for four during the Oval Test. West Indies completed a 5–0 "blackwash". August 1984

Ian Botham

ENGLAND

To an English cricket fan of a certain generation – one whose teenage years coincided with the late 1970s and early 1980s – the name Ian Botham can still make the hairs on the back of the neck stand on end. This is not to exaggerate, but then some of Botham's feats went beyond exaggeration anyway. At his peak, Botham was The Man – a raucous, bullocking, irresistible bundle of energy who could hit the ball out of the ground, swing it round corners and catch it with deceptive languor. England regarded him as a hero (the former England coach David Lloyd reckoned he was a "superhero"), and his singlehanded destruction of Australia in 1981 is part of cricket's mythology.

Rarely has a young cricketer made such an impact so quickly. In his first seven Tests he took five five-wicket hauls, including eight for 34 against Pakistan at Lord's, and hit three centuries. He reached Test cricket's double of 100 wickets and 1000 runs in 21 matches – fewer than anyone in the history of the game. And at Bombay in 1979–80 he became the first player to score a century and take 10 wickets in the same Test.

Statistics, though, were simply an affirmation of a primal instinct. Botham developed an aura – especially against Australia – which meant that bad balls often took wickets and miscues went for four. When a back problem restricted his effectiveness as an awayswing bowler in the final quarter of his career, he drew on reserves of sheer personality instead. For that was his great strength: Botham inspired the belief that something was just around the corner. While he was at the crease, or had the ball in his hand, anything seemed possible. It wasn't always but, well, there was no harm in trying. Some of Botham's low points – resigning the captaincy just before his heroics in 1981, a drugs ban in 1986, countless pieces of tabloid tittle-tattle – were as emotionally charged as his triumphs, but that summed up the man. Life in the fast lane was always preferable to the middle of the road.

TESTS	ONE–DAY INTERNATIONALS
1977–1992	*1976–1992*
Caps 102	**Caps** 116
Runs 5,200 @ 33.54	**Runs** 2,113 @ 23.21
HS 208	**HS** 79 **SR** 79.10
100s 14 **50s** 22	**50s** 9
Wkts 383 @ 28.40	**Wkts** 145 @ 28.54
BB 8/34 **5ws** 27	**BB** 4/31 **R/O** 3.96
Capt W0 L4 D8	**Capt** W4 L5

Botham the bowler sends down another delivery, seam bolt upright, against Australia at Old Trafford. August 1981

RIGHT Rod Marsh waits more in hope than expectation as Botham hits out during his epic 149 not out at Headingley. July 1981

FAR LEFT Batting without a helmet, Botham hooks for four on his way to a raucous 138 in the opening Test of the 1986–7 Ashes at Brisbane. November 1986

LEFT In his final year as an international cricketer Botham finds the energy for another appeal for leg-before in a one-day game against Pakistan at The Oval. May 1992

Geoff Boycott is tickled pink at the England team's Christmas party in Delhi. December 1981

Richard Hadlee

NEW ZEALAND

Graham Gooch once observed, only partly in jest, that batting against New Zealand was a case of facing Richard Hadlee at one end and Ilford 2nds at the other, which was probably a bit harsh on Ilford 2nds. For the best part of 15 years until his retirement in 1990, Hadlee carried a mediocre attack all by himself, eventually retiring with a then-world record 431 Test wickets, not to mention a useful tally of 3124 runs. With very little help at the other end – next in the New Zealand pantheon comes Chris Cairns with 218 – he had to work hard for his wickets. And in a country obsessed with the All Blacks he had to work harder than players from other nations to gain recognition.

Not that his silky action ever appeared to be hard work at all. Hadlee began life as a tearaway fast bowler, desperate to copy the raw brilliance of his idol, Dennis Lillee. But a drop in pace merely concentrated his talents, and he was soon making fools of the best players with a cerebral mix of leg-cutters, slower balls and yorkers.

Hadlee admitted that he was driven by statistics, but his various captains were not complaining and there were moments when he was unplayable. At Brisbane in November 1985 he took 15 Australian wickets, including a first-innings haul of nine for 52. Had he not himself caught Geoff Lawson, he would surely have claimed all 10. Five-fors littered his CV: there were 36 in Tests, to go with nine 10-wicket hauls – another record until Muttiah Muralitharan began to bamboozle opponents on a regular basis.

Yet it was remarkable that Hadlee got as far as he did. In the mid-1980s he suffered a mental and physical breakdown and was rescued only by a stubborn adherence to the tenets of positive thought. It was an approach that reaped rewards until the very end. In his final Test appearance, against England at Edgbaston at the age of 39, he removed Devon Malcolm with the 21,918th and last ball of his Test career to finish with five for 53. It had been one of the easiest of his 431 wickets. But no one could say he hadn't earned it.

TESTS
1973–1990
Caps 86
Runs 3,124 @ 27.16
HS 151*
100s 2 **50s** 15
Wkts 431 @ 22.29
BB 9/52 **5ws** 36

ONE-DAY INTERNATIONALS
1973–1990
Caps 115
Runs 1,751 @ 21.61
HS 79 **SR** 75.50
50s 4
Wkts 158 @ 21.61
BB 5/25 **R/O** 3.30

Lost in thought at
The Oval, possibly
contemplating his
18 years as an
international cricketer.
May 1990

RIGHT One of the
images of our times: an
X-shaped Hadlee
appeals for yet another
leg-before decision,
against India at
Mumbai. He inspired
New Zealand to victory
by 136 runs.
November 1988

Muttiah Muralitharan

SRI LANKA

No team in the history of the game has been more indebted to a single player than Sri Lanka to Muttiah Muralitharan. When he made his Test debut in August 1992, they had won only two of their first 37 Tests. In the 12 years since then, they won 36 out of 111 and made the journey from the realm of pushovers to the land of movers and shakers.

Their not-so-secret weapon has been Muralitharan, a small, shy son of a confectioner with the ability to fool batsmen at will and put a collective smile on the face of his 20 million compatriots – something only he was capable of doing when he played a prominent role in the tsunami relief effort. Not everyone is convinced that his unique brand of wristy off-spin is legal, but not even the whispers of opponents and the whims of Australian umpires can detract from his achievements. While the debate goes on, Murali has continued to do what he does best: bowling his big-turning off-breaks with accuracy, mischief and goggle-eyed concentration – and dismissing batsmen by the bucketload.

He is the lifeblood of the Sri Lankan attack, taking nearly two-fifths of their wickets since his debut, and he is likely to end his career with a wicket tally that might never be broken. In August 1998 at The Oval he famously chiselled away at England's batting line-up to finish with match figures of 16 for 220, including nine for 65 in the second innings. And in January 2002, against Zimbabwe in his home town of Kandy, he was a dropped catch away from achieving the best analysis in all Test cricket, settling for a return of nine for 51 instead. But as well as rewriting record books, Murali has helped to change trends, carrying the game away from the pace-dominated 1980s into a more subtle era, one in which phrases like the "doosra" (Hindi for "second" or the "other one") have become part of cricket's terminology. Together with his great rival Shane Warne he helped make spin sexy again, and the whole of Sri Lanka worships him for it.

LEFT **The eye has it: Muttiah Muralitharan and his infectious smile. December 2002**

TESTS
1992–2004
Caps 91
Runs 942 @ 12.56
HS 67
50s 1
Wkts 532 @ 22.86
BB 9/51 **5ws** 44

ONE-DAY INTERNATIONALS
1993–2004
Caps 237
Runs 385 @ 5.92
HS 19 **SR** 67.90
Wkts 366 @ 22.13
BB 7/30 **R/O** 3.77

Mobbed by team-mates on his way to match figures of 16 for 220 against England at The Oval. Sri Lanka won by 10 wickets – their first Test victory in England. August 1998

On the charge after
bowling West Indies'
Ricardo Powell for a
single during a World
Cup group game at
Cape Town. Sri Lanka
won by six runs and
went on to reach the
semi-finals.
February 2003

The contorted mouth
reveals the concentration
as Murali bowls during
the Edgbaston Test
against England.
May 2002

Grinning again, this
time at a calendar of
caricatures during
the World Cup in
South Africa.
March 2003

Imran Khan

PAKISTAN

Imran Khan was the natural successor to the virile Australian all-rounder Keith Miller. He batted with a flourish, bowled with panache and charmed the socks – and possibly more – off women. He was a sex symbol with film-star looks and a hauteur that could repel and attract in equal measure. Pakistani cricket had never seen anything like him, although quite often they didn't see anything of him either: he went to Oxford University in 1973 and had spells with Worcestershire and Sussex, immersing himself in western culture and enjoying the bachelor lifestyle.

Following his retirement he married, then divorced, Jemima Goldsmith, a high-society girl half his age, and moved inevitably into politics. But he was also a dazzling cricketer who got better with age. His final deed on the field of play was to hold aloft the 1992 World Cup on a balmy night in Melbourne – the alpha-male in his element, unconcerned that he was just a few months away from turning 40.

Imran's natural ebullience was reflected in his bowling: a gliding run followed by an explosion at the crease that catapulted him high into the air. He helped make fast-bowling fashionable in a part of the world where spin was usually king, and is generally credited with deciphering the mysteries of reverse-swing, a legacy used to devastating effect by two of his proteges, Wasim Akram and Waqar Younis.

Natural wear and tear prompted an inevitable drop in pace, but his figures improved – in both bowling and batting. In the last 10 years of his Test career, Imran averaged a barely believable 19 with the ball and almost 50 with the bat. By the time he finally retired, after a couple of false alarms, he could claim to be the best batsman of the four great all-rounders who fought out their own private battles throughout the 1980s: Ian Botham, Richard Hadlee, Kapil Dev and Imran himself.

But it was his inspirational leadership of Pakistan's World Cup team that lingered in the memory. Exhorting a struggling side that was on the brink of elimination to fight like cornered tigers, Imran not only coined a phrase but also lifted a nation. A heart-throb and pretty talented too – some people have all the luck.

TESTS
1971–1992
Caps 88
Runs 3,807 @ 37.69
HS 136
100s 6 50s 18
Wkts 362 @ 22.81
BB 8/58 5ws 23
Capt W14 L8 D26

ONE-DAY INTERNATIONALS
1974–1992
Caps 175
Runs 3,709 @ 33.41
HS 102* SR 72.64
100s 1 50s 19
Wkts 182 @ 26.61
BB 6/14 R/O 3.89
Capt W75 L59 T1 NR4

Shane Warne

AUSTRALIA

Debuts can be deceptive. It was January 1992 and a tubby, 22-year-old leg-spinner was being spanked around the Sydney Cricket Ground by India's batsmen. Shane Warne finished with figures of one for 150, and after three Tests his bowling average stood at 335. Had he been English he would probably have been dropped for good, but the Australian selectors have always known their own minds and gave him another chance. It was to prove one of the canniest decisions in the history of the game. A match-winning burst in Colombo was followed by seven for 52 against West Indies at Melbourne, but it was not until Warne's wonderball to Mike Gatting at Old Trafford in June 1993, his first delivery in Ashes cricket, that the penny dropped. Here was a star in the making. He had the strut, the pout, the theatrical oohs and aahs and a tendency to make headlines for reasons other than cricket.

And, boy, could he bowl: after a misleadingly gentle three-step approach came an explosion at the crease, a muscular whirl of the right shoulder and a fizzing, dipping leg-break, or sometimes a laser-guided flipper. He would work out a batsman as if he were a mathematical equation, thinking, probing, testing, until – Eureka! At the end of the decade he was selected as one of Wisden's Five Cricketers of the Century, having administered the kiss of life to leg-spin, a trade which was drowning in a sea of pacemen.

More than that, Warne took leg-spin to a new level. It had always been considered an attractive but profligate art, dangerous but costly. Warne combined penetration with economy, which is every captain's dream, and became the focal point of the rampaging Australian team of the mid-to-late 1990s. Young boys could suddenly be seen bowling out of the back of their hands in the park. Not even a one-year ban for taking diuretics could stop the revolution, and Warne returned in 2004 to claim the world record for most Test wickets. You couldn't have written the script. No wonder his team-mates call him Hollywood.

LEFT Warne has always had a persuasive way with umpires. Here he tries to win another decision against Pakistan at Hobart. November 1999

TESTS
1992–2004
Caps 119
Runs 2,449 @ 16.21
HS 99
100s 0 **50s** 9
Wkts 561 @ 25.50
BB 8/71 **5ws** 28

ONE-DAY INTERNATIONALS
1993–2003
Caps 193
Runs 1,016 @ 13.02
HS 55 **SR** 72.00
100s 0 **50s** 1
Wkts 291 @ 25.82
BB 5/33 **R/O** 4.25
Capt W10 L1 T0 NR0

Ever the showman, Warne tries to distract the English batsman with a spot of face-pulling at The Oval. August 1993

Imploring the umpire
to come round to his
way of thinking against
England in the sixth
Test at The Oval.
August 1997

Australia have just
whitewashed New
Zealand 3–0 at
Adelaide, so there's
plenty to smile about.
November 2004

RIGHT Celebrating after
trapping Curtly
Ambrose lbw during
Australia's World Cup
win over West Indies at
Old Trafford.
May 1999

Sachin Tendulkar

INDIA

TESTS
1989–2004
Caps 120
Runs 9,879 @ 57.43
HS 248*
100s 34 **50s** 38
Wkts 36 @ 47.25
BB 3/10 **5ws** 0
Capt W4 L9 D12

ONE-DAY INTERNATIONALS
1989–2004
Caps 342
Runs 13,497 @ 44.84
HS 186* **SR** 86.20
100s 37 **50s** 69
Wkts 132 @ 44.07
BB 5/32 **R/O** 5.03
Capt W23 L43 T1 NR6

Ask any tuk-tuk driver in any city in India. Sachin Tendulkar is more than a cricketer. He is a brand, an institution, a phenomenon. In the eyes of some of his fans, he is little less than a god. Tendulkar has cherubic curly hair, boyish looks and the nickname "Little Master", yet the burden he carries to the crease each innings is like that of no other batsman in the history of the game. Millions and millions expect him to score runs for India. To be in his home town of Mumbai when he fails is to intrude on private grief, as if a loved one has died. It is fortunate, then, that Tendulkar has given his people plenty to smile about.

When Sir Donald Bradman first saw him on television, he called his wife over to watch. Bradman had spotted something of himself in the young Sachin and included him in his own all-time XI, published only after his death. And when, in 2002, Tendulkar made his 30th Test hundred to pass Bradman's own tally, another Indian legend, Sunil Gavaskar, declared that he was "probably the most complete batsman the game has seen".

If the hyperbole was in danger of getting out of hand, then the numbers were beginning to do the same: a total of 23,376 runs in Tests and one-day internationals, with 71 hundreds – way ahead of his nearest rivals – and 107 fifties by the end of 2004. In a country that has sometimes valued individual landmarks more than team success, Tendulkar is near-perfection itself. He plays beautifully too. At the age of 17 he made a brave undefeated 119 to save India from defeat against England in a Test match at Old Trafford, but guts and determination are only a tiny part of it. Tendulkar can time a delivery through midwicket from outside off-stump with no more than a flick of the wrists, and his cover-driving is a thing of rare beauty. Above all, though, he has got "it" – that indefinable quality that fills stadia when he is in, and threatens to empty them, especially in India, when he is out.

Cutting insouciantly against England in the second Test at Trent Bridge, where Tendulkar made 34 and 92.
August 2002

LEFT A rare moment of relaxation for Tendulkar after India have beaten Pakistan in the first Test at Multan.
April 2004

Tendulkar thanks the heavens for reaching three figures against Pakistan at Multan. He went on to make 194 not out as India won by an innings and 52 runs. March 2004

Adam Gilchrist watches
as Tendulkar helps the
ball to leg during the
epic draw with Australia
at Sydney.
January 2004

Andrew Flintoff

ENGLAND

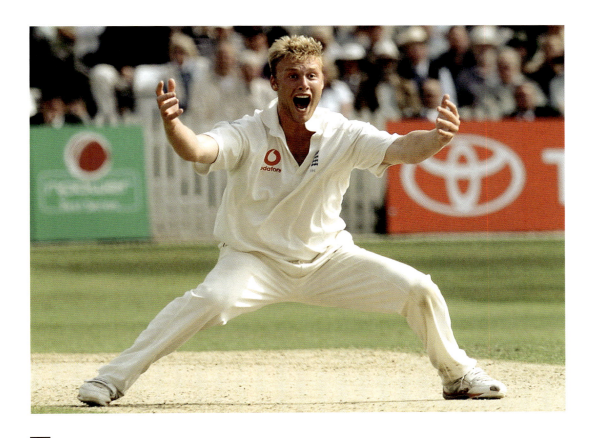

LEFT Grinning all the way to the pavilion: Flintoff has just taken 104 off Sri Lanka during the ICC Champions Trophy – his third one-day century in six innings. September 2004

ABOVE Imploring the umpire to uphold an appeal for lbw against New Zealand's Nathan Astle at Trent Bridge. Flintoff won his shout – and Astle was out for 0. June 2004

The smile said it all. Andrew Flintoff had just been dismissed for 99, aiming for his hundred with another big hit, during a NatWest Challenge game against India in September 2004. But instead of frowning back to the Oval pavilion, he grinned the whole way. It was pure Flintoff: selfless, instinctive, untroubled. And in any case, what was there not to smile about?

In the space of no time at all, the all-rounder known as Freddie had become the hero English cricket had been crying out for since the retirement of Ian Botham. Blond, broad and with a gait that was somewhere between gentle giant and marauding viking, Flintoff spent most of England's golden summer of 2004 launching sixes and – when he didn't quite connect with the ball – the occasional four. There were 37 boundary-clearing hits in all, each one lifted with the ease of a man tossing salad and greeted by cheers from crowds who could hardly believe what they were seeing.

It was simple: this was Flintoff, the people's cricketer, doing what came naturally. Groans when England lost a wicket quickly gave way to raucous anticipation if it meant he was the next man in. Flintoff had always shown promise. Now, finally, he was realising it. To see his destructive 167 against West Indies at Edgbaston was to witness a man who had come to terms with his game. It had not always been thus. In his younger days, Flintoff was accused of carrying too much weight. But as the beer gave way to cranberry juice, so his game moved from fast-food to cordon bleu.

His batting, always his stronger suit, underwent an epiphany in Colombo in December 2003, when his patient 77 hinted at a more mature gameplan. His bowling developed too – from short-of-a-length Scrooge to wicket-taking enforcer. It is virtually impossible to dislike Flintoff: his enthusiasm is infectious and his smile has been noted in all corners of cricket's globe. For years during the 1980s and 90s England's performances drove their fans to the bars in search of solace. To the consternation of catering managers everywhere, Flintoff pulled them in the other direction.

TESTS
1998–2004
Caps 42
Runs 2,107 @ 32.92
HS 167
100s 4 **50s** 13
Wkts 95 @ 36.60
BB 5/58 **5ws** 1

ONE-DAY INTERNATIONALS
1999–2004
Caps 80
Runs 2,111 @ 35.18
HS 123 **SR** 92.95
100s 3 **50s** 13
Wkts 82 @ 23.97
BB 4/14 **R/O** 4.20

Waiting to bat against
Sri Lanka in Colombo.
December 2003

Few big men have been
as athletic as Flintoff,
fielding here against
West Indies at The Oval.
August 2004

Duck! Mowing to leg during a punishing 58 against West Indies in the first Test at Lord's. July 2004.

Chapter Seven

The Future

It's March 2013, and tension is mounting during the third and deciding Ashes Test at Sharjah. Australia's middle-order rock Michael Clarke is speaking breathlessly into the mic on his collar, trying to convince the vast TV audience in India that he just grounded his bat in time. But Ian Bell's argument – that his direct hit from cover point deserves recognition – is persuasive, if not entirely based on logic. As the votes pour in, piling up in the top left corner of the TV screen, it is clear that Clarke is in trouble. In fact, he is out – by two whole percentage points! Bell's throw might not have beaten Clarke's lunge, but these days it's the fans who hold sway, not the humdrum reality of feet and inches. As Clarke shakes his head, Bell gives a smiling thumbs-up to the cameras, and has 30 seconds to thank the public while the next batsman is driven in a golf buggy to the crease by the MD of the series sponsors. England go on to win the game, thus claiming their first Ashes triumph for 27 years, and announce that they are looking forward to defending the urn in Singapore in three months' time.

Complete science-fiction? Or a sneak preview of the game's future, a place where technology and the people rule, and cricket's power base has shifted to the subcontinent? Cricket has always been so full of surprises that nothing can be discounted, not even England winning the Ashes. Who, after all, would have predicted the epoch-making impact of World Series Cricket? Or the way Hawkeye has changed our perspective of lbw decisions? Or that cricket would turn to baseball for advice on how to throw? Or that a 20-over slog would be hailed as the game's saviour?

Change is inevitable, especially in those parts of the game that have resisted it for so long. We have already seen how the commercial attractiveness of the Indian market has given birth to numerous one-day internationals to keep satellite television happy and the bank balances of the national boards healthy. But the pulling power of the masses is spreading, and in 2003 it spread into that most unexpected of environments: the English county circuit. Twenty20 is barely out of its nappies (coloured, of course), but already a generation of county chief executives are wondering: how did we ever get by without it?

To be at Lord's on July 15, 2004 was to ask the same question yourself. The ground is often referred to as cricket's HQ, but had missed out on staging a Twenty20 game in 2003 because the local council was concerned about the musical jingles that accompany everything from wickets to boundaries to incoming batsmen. But when Middlesex hosted their London rivals Surrey, the spectators turned out in their thousands. The attendance figure of 26,500 was the highest at the ground for a non-cup-final county game in over 50 years, and the demographics hinted at a brave new world: everyone was there, from City workers to schoolchildren to – whisper it – young women. And the signs are that the growth has only just begun. In 2004, a total of 286,000 spectators watched Twenty20 Cup matches in England, which represented a 12% rise on the previous year. A further 27 group games have been added to county cricket's fixture list for 2005 and more expansion is planned. The bug is spreading. Officials in South Africa were delighted when crowds flocked to watch what they called the Pro20 Series in the early part of 2004, because domestic cricket in that country has, since the end of the isolation years at least, been even more poorly supported than in England. And Sri Lanka held its own two-day Twenty20 championship in September last year.

But perhaps the most exciting aspect of the Twenty20 revolution is that, like a precocious batsman,

LEFT Australia's Andy Bichel looks like The Bionic Man as he has his bowling action monitored by sensors during a training session in Perth. October 2003

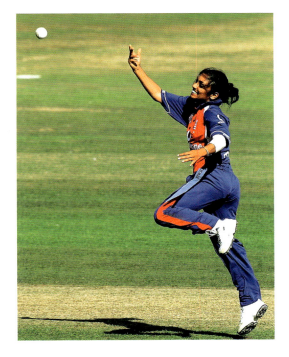

England's Isa Guha celebrates after taking a return catch against New Zealand at Hove in The NatWest Women's Series. August 2004

Perth's pylons provide the only ray of light at a one-day international between Australia and Sri Lanka at the WACA. December 2002

it did not take long to make the step up from domestic level. Last August at Hove, England's women met New Zealand to contest the first NatWest Twenty20 international, so maintaining a short but proud tradition of beating the men to it (the women staged their first World Cup in 1973, the men in 1975). But this tentative dip of the toe could well lead to full-scale immersion. In February this year, New Zealand hosted Australia at Auckland for the first men's Twenty20 international, and Australia's first international fixture in this summer's Ashes series is a Twenty20 match against England at Hampshire's Rose Bowl on June 13. Years ago, this abbreviated version of the game would have been derided as hit-and-giggle cricket. Now, there is even talk of staging a Twenty20 World Cup. After years of mainly unsuccessful attempts to convince the public that cricket below international level is worth paying for, the sport might just have struck gold.

So will Twenty20 leave other forms of the game wheezing in its wake? Test cricket will be fine as long as it continues to pack out stadiums in England, Australia and, to a lesser extent, India, even if there are concerns that Australia's monopoly will drive

punters away. If anything, it is the money-spinning one-day international that might now have to look at itself in the mirror. Critics argue that Twenty20 takes the best bits of the 50-over game (the beginning and the end) and ditches the regimented middle overs, when batsmen work the ball around for singles against spinners and medium-pacers. If the Twenty20 World Cup really does happen, then the conventional World Cup could be the first casualty.

The role of technology is likely to become increasingly central, despite the traditionalists' view that umpires are being reduced to hat-stands. But the argument that human flaws are part of the game's charm – that umpires should be allowed to make mistakes – is no longer sustainable in an age where every decision is replayed so many times and studied from so many angles that the armchair viewer develops a kind of helpless omniscience, while the umpire just develops a kind of helplessness. With players' careers at stake and media analysis at an all-time critical high, it cannot be right that the only person who isn't sure whether the batsman got a nick to short leg via his front pad is the one who is paid to make the decision.

In fact, technology's inevitable incursion into the decision-making process of the game has been going on for some time as the ICC seeks to lessen the burden on the men in white. TV replays for line-decisions (run-outs and stumpings) are now routine, as are referrals to the third umpire to check whether a catch has been taken cleanly, although in many cases not even TV is the all-seeing eye it sometimes claims to be. At the ICC Champions Trophy in 2002–3, umpires were even allowed to ask their TV-box colleague to adjudicate on lbws: had the ball pitched in line with the stumps, and did the batsman get an inside edge? Pakistan's Shoaib Malik was the first victim, but the experiment did not continue: it was felt that too much time was needed to refer the decision, and that an element of subjectivity remained. At the Champions Trophy in 2004, umpires used earpieces that both allowed them to communicate directly with the TV umpire – who assumed the responsibility for calling no-balls – and pick up any noises on the stump microphone which might help them with caught-behind decisions.

As far as the fan is concerned, however, the most innovative piece of gadgetry has been Hawkeye, an ingenious tracking device which uses images processed by several cameras around the ground to predict the path of the ball. First used by the English TV company Channel 4 in 2001, Hawkeye added a new dimension to the cricket-watching experience, even if sceptics were unconvinced it was able to master the subtleties of swing and spin. Even so, it has at least succeeded in involving the viewers, inviting them to make the decision themselves and, more often than not, think twice before they hurl abuse at the umpire. It is a level of interactivity that is being mirrored more and more inside the stadiums too: the day when the spectators rule on Bell's run-out of Clarke might not be so fantastical.

As the high-profile, televised matches – mainly internationals – adopt fresh new gimmicks to appeal to new fans, so the sport at domestic level will have to adapt too. Twenty20 suggests there is hope, but more needs to be done, particularly in England, where a professional structure that supports over 400 first-class cricketers and is financially reliant on the England and Wales Cricket Board has never been short of snipers. "I am sure that most people agree that fewer county matches would mean better cricket," wrote the Wisden editor Wilfrid H Brookes. That was in 1937, but his concern could apply equally to 2005. Various solutions have been mooted: a move away from big-name but empty stadiums to the more idyllic, atmospheric, and better-supported outgrounds; a reduction in the number of counties; a reduction in the number of competitions; even the abolition of the county system altogether in favour of a city- and town-based structure, as in football and rugby.

The international game will change too, more so off the field than on it, since only Kenya have even the faintest hope of becoming the 11th Test nation, and their progress has been stunted by infighting and allegations of match-fixing. No, the seismic shifts are more likely to occur in the boardroom, where the subcontinent – and India in particular – grows ever stronger, confident in the knowledge that its TV deals will continue to generate huge sums of money for the game. The old axis of England and Australia is slowly losing its cachet, and in 2005 the ICC confirmed it would be moving its headquarters away from Lord's to Dubai in the United Arab Emirates – a change of scenery that is ostensibly for tax purposes, but which also carries huge symbolic significance.

The Middle East's place in cricket's consciousness has already been established by the annual one-day competition in Sharjah, which also hosted two Tests between Pakistan and West Indies in the early part of 2002 because of fears of terrorist attacks on the subcontinent after the events of September 11. But Dubai will take the association a step further in 2007 with the planned opening of the first Global Cricket Academy, run by the ICC and based in Dubai Sports City, the world's first purpose-built sporting metropolis. The hope is that Dubai's central location will help attract promising young cricketers from all the over the world: not just from the 10 Test teams plus Kenya, who have special one-day international status, but from the other 81 member countries of the ICC.

Ultimately, though, plotting cricket's future is as subjective as wallowing in its past. Some reports have suggested that the next superpower in the sport will be China, which at least tallies with the general movement of cricket's soul towards the east. But wherever it is played, one thing is pretty much guaranteed: the surprises will never stop.

And they said the Americans would never join the club! USA fans at the ICC Champions Trophy. September 2004

Light, camera, action. Well, two out of three isn't bad as the TV men film the players' football-style dugout during a Twenty20 Cup match.
June 2003

The England coach Duncan Fletcher faces the press at the Kolkata Cricket and Football Club.
January 2002

At last, a plan to slow
down Australia's express
Brett Lee, who tests his
aerodynamism during
a training session in
Potchefstroom,
South Africa.
February 2003

The bird's-eye view
from the NatWest
media centre at Lord's,
where Australia are
taking on Pakistan
in the final of the
World Cup.
June 1999

Practising the mow over
long-on as part of the
NatWest Inter Cricket
initiative during a
NatWest Challenge
game between
England and Pakistan
at Old Trafford.
June 2003

Fans raise a pint to the first Twenty20 Cup game to be staged at Lord's. A near-capacity crowd of 26,500 cheered on the London derby between Middlesex and Surrey. July 2004

The Western Warriors
wicket-keeper Ryan
Campbell looks like an
extra in *Star Wars* as
his side take on the
Queensland Bulls in
the final of Australia's
ING Cup.
February 2004

Dave Houghton (left)
and David Gower burn
the candle at one end to
bring Sky TV's audience
commentary of the
inaugural NatWest
Series game between
West Indies and
Zimbabwe at Bristol.
July 2000

It's Hong Kong in
September, so it must
be the Hong Kong Sixes
– an annual slogfest
attracting top-class
teams from all over
the world.
September 1997

Chapter Eight

Extras

If golf is a good walk spoiled, as Mark Twain once claimed, then where does that leave cricket? A long-irrelevant tool for empire-building? An extended in-joke occasionally too serious for its own good? Or an entrancing spectacle diluted by moments of sheer absurdity? Cricket is all these things – and a lot more. It is a sport, a pastime, a passion, an obsession, a mountain, a molehill, a whim and a fancy. It matters deeply, and it matters not a jot. And because the game in its highest form takes place over such a leisurely period – a Test match lasts as long as the working week, and can leave you feeling even more drained – it encourages dreamers and idealists, streakers and fancy-dress aficionados, all of them with far too much time on their hands.

Rudyard Kipling might have mocked "the flannelled fools at the wicket", but he seemed to reserve harsher words for the "muddied oafs at the goals". For no other sport is as endearing in its ability to attract the curious and the idiosyncratic as cricket. In what other game can you be caught at silly point off a googly for a duck? And in what other game would two senior BBC radio commentators be permitted to giggle for several minutes live on air because one of them had explained that the dismissal of Ian Botham had occurred because he "couldn't quite get his leg over?" Cricket can be the stuff of freemasonry, but once you are in on the secret it all seems so obvious. And so magnificently, gloriously, self-indulgently pointless.

Yet that is a huge part of its charm, and sometimes the game can be just as entertaining when it's not actually taking place. "Rain stops play" is a familiar enough headline to cricket fans, but it is also the thin end of a wonderfully unpredictable wedge. A domestic match in India between Tamil Nadu and Punjab was once interrupted by a snake on the outfield, followed later in the match by a swarm of bees. And in 2003, a flock of 200 squawking seagulls got in the way of Glamorgan's attempts to host Surrey at Cardiff. On other occasions, it hasn't even needed animals or insects to stick their noses and wings in. The game between Worcestershire and Sri Lanka "A" at New Road in 1999 was held up by the solar eclipse. But surely the most bizarre hiatus in recent times occurred when the Border batsman Daryll Cullinan hit a six into a spectator's pan of fried calamari in a game against Boland at Paarl, South Africa, in 1995, causing play to be held up for 10 minutes while the sizzling ball cooled down.

If that incident gave new meaning to the term "audience participation", then it was merely part of a time-honoured tradition. At the fall of a wicket during a one-day game at Derby, a member of the public strode to the crease and was allowed to face a joke delivery before he was escorted off the field. The same thing almost happened during the 2001 Headingley Test between England and Australia, although the prankster in question didn't quite achieve his aim of facing a ball from Glenn McGrath or Jason Gillespie. And, as security has tightened, streakers have been forced to keep their clothes on, often in the form of fancy dress. These days it's a toss-up as to which you'll spot first upon arriving at the Test: three male nuns, five Elvis Presleys, or 11 international cricketers.

Cricket's tendency to lurch from the sublime to the ridiculous knows no bounds, yet it continues to inspire devotion beyond the call of duty. The final word must go to the fan in Melbourne who was arrested in 1999 for selling drugs to feed his cricket memorabilia habit. When police found a stash of cannabis at his home, they also came across bats signed by Don Bradman and Brian Lara. The notion that great batting can leave the observer on a high never felt quite right after that.

Sri Lanka's Tillekeratne Dilshan could do some with a few tips about how to fly a kite during the second Test against England at Kandy. December 2003

LEFT Lord's – pristine in white. January 2003

England's fielders in India don't seem to be too disconcerted at taking their drinks break in what looks like a miniature space shuttle. February 1993

Happy days for Phil Tufnell, who indulges in his favourite pastime at Southgate as his team-mate Mike Roseberry looks on. July 2000

An Air New Zealand plane takes off under the shadows of the Remarkables mountain range in Queenstown, Otago, where England are preparing for the first Test.
March 2002

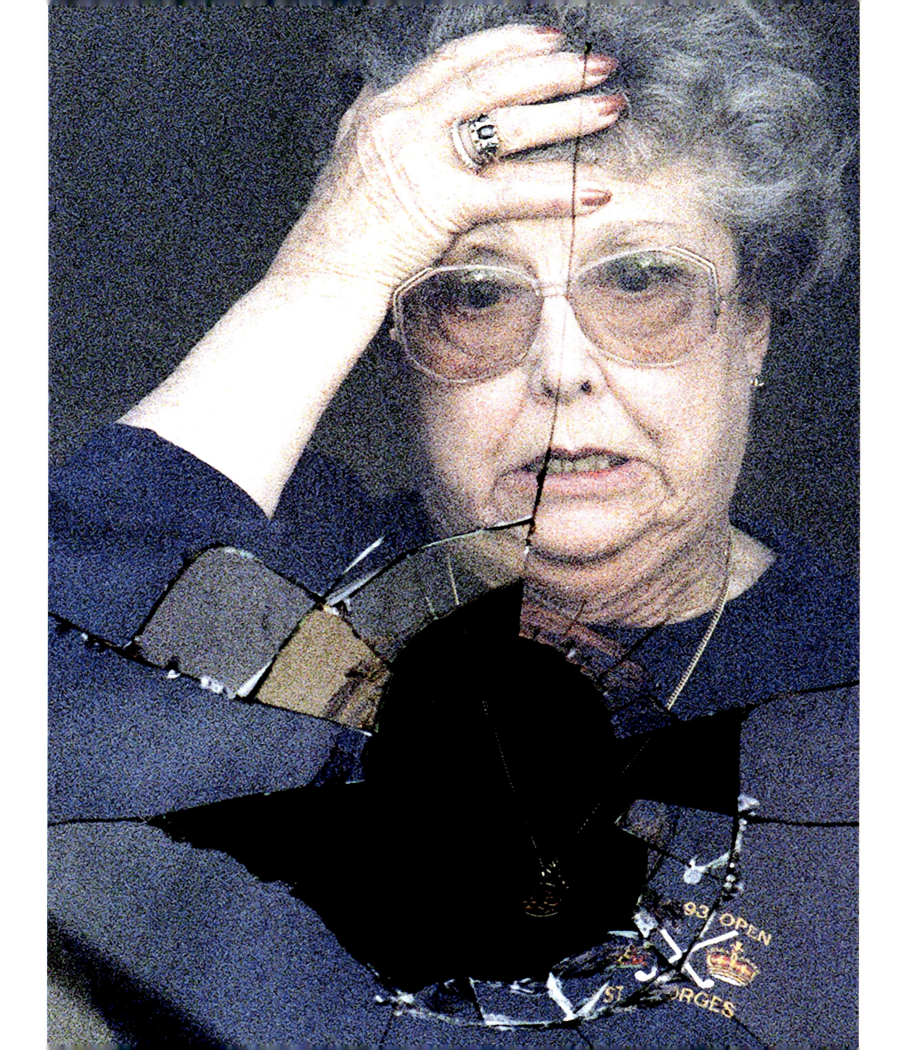

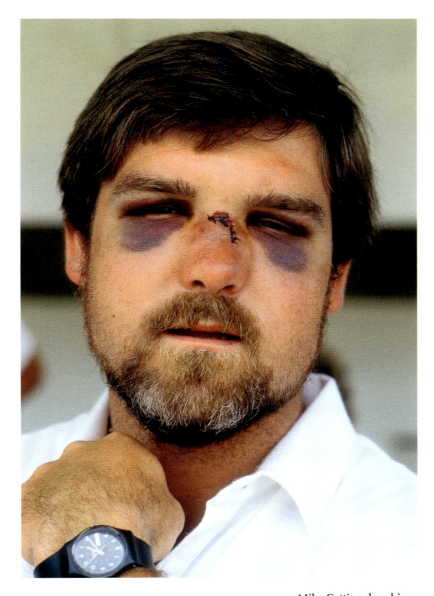

Left What have they done? A Hove resident inspects the damage after Paul Jarvis connects just a little too well with a six.
May 1996

Mike Gatting does his best panda impression after being hit in the face by a Malcolm Marshall bouncer during the first one-day international between West Indies and England at Sabina Park in Jamaica.
February 1986

The blazer is
unmistakably that of the
Marylebone Cricket
Club. The belly – and
the newspaper – go with
the territory.
July 2004

The former England
captain Rachael
Heyhoe-Flint (centre)
leads the celebrations
after the MCC admits
its first 10 women
members.
September 1998

Cricket whites take on a different connotation during a one-day international between West Indies and Australia in Trinidad.
May 2003

Fans of the Sully Centurions blend into the background during the Village Cup final at Lord's.
August 2004

Spectators spy more
rain as the fourth Test
between England and
India at The Oval falls
foul of the weather.
September 2002

Five Elvis reincarnates
strut their stuff
at Adelaide.
November 2002

The wicketkeeper appeals for a stumping during a match at Roedean School in Brighton. May 1996

Mandie Godliman goes up for lbw against India's Anjum Chopra during a one-day international at Beaconsfield. The umpire said not out, but England still won by six wickets. August 2002

RIGHT The padlock says it all. January 2003

ENGLAND

AUTOGRAPH COLLECTING

Room Attendants have been instructed not to accept Autograph Books, Bats etc. for the purpose of obtaining Players' Autographs.

To prevent embarrassment, it is requested that Attendants not be approached for this purpose.

AUSTRALIA

	BOWLERS	WKTS	RUNS
1	McGRATH	2	3 2
2	GILLESPIE	2	4 1
3	KASPROWICZ	2	3 9
4	WARNE	2	7 9
5	LEHMANN	2	4 6

The scoreboard in Adelaide reveals that two's company during the second Test between Australia and New Zealand. November 2004

The scoreboard at the
P. Saravanamuttu
Stadium in Colombo
tells the tale of a rare
Australian collapse
during the first Test
against Pakistan,
scheduled in Sri Lanka
because of security
fears. No matter:
Australia won anyway.
October 2002

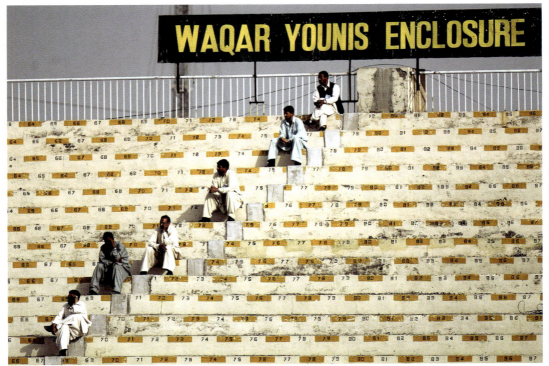

It's clear which is the
best angle to watch a
training session in
Rawalpindi's Waqar
Younis Enclosure.
March 2004

Graeme Hick tries to
remember which piece
of equipment he left in
the dressing-room.
1989

Sometimes it all came
just a little bit too easily
for Viv Richards.
June 1988

The New Zealand
umpire Billy Bowden
isn't being lifted into
the air by a crane. He's
signalling a six.
July 2004

Charlie Dagnall of the
Leicestershire Foxes
practises his gurning
technique during a
Twenty20 match.
July 2004

Four pieces of wood –
cricket's a simple
game really.
June 1995

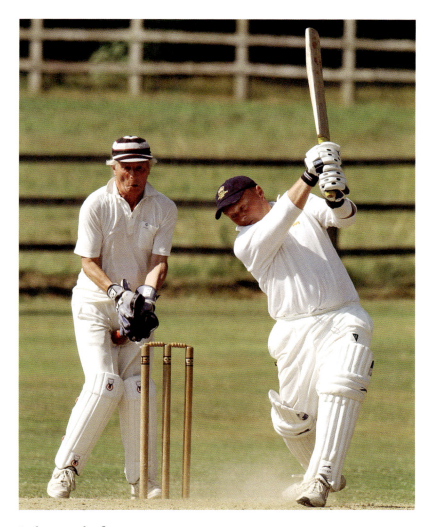

In the grounds of
Windsor Castle, a
wicketkeeper winces as
the ball strikes him in
the area of the body
known in the trade
as "amidships."
July 2003

Cricket on ice in
St Moritz, Switzerland.
February 2001

An impromptu game
of cricket on the beach
in Barbados.
April 2004

Statistics

All statistics apply to games from the beginning of 1980 to the end of 2004

Tests

Most Runs

SR Waugh	10,927
BC Lara	10,094
AR Border	10,072
SR Tendulkar	9,879
AJ Stewart	8,463
GA Gooch	8,146
ME Waugh	8,029
MA Atherton	7,728
MA Taylor	7,525
DC Boon	7,422

Most Wickets

SK Warne	561
M Muralitharan	532
CA Walsh	519
GD McGrath	477
A Kumble	444
Wasim Akram	414
CEL Ambrose	405
MD Marshall	373
Waqar Younis	373
SM Pollock	361

Most Catches/Stumpings

IA Healy	395
MV Boucher	290
AC Gilchrist	278
AJ Stewart	277
PJL Dujon	272
RD Jacobs	219
AC Parore	204
ME Waugh	181
IDS Smith	176
RC Russell	165

Most Appearances

SR Waugh	168
AR Border	142
AJ Stewart	133
CA Walsh	132
ME Waugh	128
SR Tendulkar	120
IA Healy	119
SK Warne	119
MA Atherton	115
DL Haynes	112
BC Lara	112

Best Ecomony Rates

WJ Cronje	2.03
Mohammad Nazir	2.10
RA Harper	2.14
JV Coney	2.14
NJ Astle	2.20
Iqbal Qasim	2.22
Arshad Khan	2.23
EJ Chatfield	2.23
DL Underwood	2.24
SLV Raju	2.25
HA Gomes	2.25

Best Strike Rates

Waqar Younis	43.49
Shoaib Akhtar	43.72
MD Marshall	45.88
AA Donald	47.02
Imran Khan	47.83
RJ Hadlee	47.96
MA Holding	50.39
DW Headley	50.43
LS Pascoe	50.52
GD McGrath	51.47

Best Partnerships per Wicket

1st	GC Smith & HH Gibbs	368	
	South Africa v Pakistan, Cape Town 2002/03		
2nd	RS Mahanama & ST Jayasuriya	576	
	Sri Lanka v India, Colombo (RPS) 1997		
3rd	AH Jones & MD Crowe	467	
	New Zealand v Sri Lanka, Wellington 1990/91		
4th	VVS Laxman & SR Tendulkar	353	
	India v Australia, Sydney 2003/04		
5th	SR Waugh & GS Blewett	385	
	Australia v South Africa, Johannesburg 1996/97		
6th	DR Martyn & AC Gilchrist	317	
	Australia v South Africa, Johannesburg 2001/02		
7th	Yousuf Youhana & Saqlain Mushtaq	248	
	Pakistan v New Zealand, Christchurch 2000/01		
8th	Saqlain Mushtaq & Wasim Akram	313	
	Pakistan v Zimbabwe, Sheikhupura 1996/97		
9th	PL Symcox & MV Boucher	195	
	South Africa v Pakistan, Johannesburg 1997/98		
10th	Mushtaq Ahmed & Azhar Mahmood	151	
	Pakistan v South Africa, Rawalpindi 1997/98		

Highest Individual Innings

BC Lara	400*	*West Indies v England, St John's 2003/04*
ML Hayden	380	*Australia v Zimbabwe, Perth 2003/04*
BC Lara	375	*West Indies v England, St John's 1993/94*
ST Jayasuriya	340	*Sri Lanka v India, Colombo (RPS) 1997*
MA Taylor	334*	*Australia v Pakistan, Peshawar 1998/99*
GA Gooch	333	*England v India, Lord's 1990*
Inzamam-ul-Haq	329	*Pakistan v New Zealand, Lahore 2002*
V Sehwag	309	*India v Pakistan, Multan 2003/04*
MD Crowe	299	*New Zealand v Sri Lanka, Wellington 1990/91*
VVS Laxman	281	*India v Australia, Kolkata 2000/01*

Best Bowling

A Kumble	10/74	*India v Pakistan, Delhi 1998/99*
M Muralitharan	9/51	*Sri Lanka v Zimbabwe, Kandy 2001/02*
RJ Hadlee	9/52	*New Zealand v Australia, Brisbane 1985/86*
Abdul Qadir	9/56	*Pakistan v England, Lahore 1987/88*
DE Malcolm	9/57	*England v South Africa, The Oval 1994*
M Muralitharan	9/65	*Sri Lanka v England, The Oval 1998*
Kapil Dev	9/83	*India v West Indies, Ahmedabad 1983/84*
GD McGrath	8/24	*Australia v Pakistan, Perth 2004/05*
GD McGrath	8/38	*Australia v England, Lord's 1997*
RGD Willis	8/43	*England v Australia, Leeds 1981*

Highest Team Score

Sri Lanka	952/6d	*v India, Colombo (RPS) 1997*
West Indies	751/5d	*v England, St John's 2003/04*
Australia	735/6d	*v Zimbabwe, Perth 2003/04*
Sri Lanka	713/3d	*v Zimbabwe, Bulawayo 2004*
Pakistan	708	*v England, The Oval 1987*
India	705/7d	*v Australia, Sydney 2003/04*
Pakistan	699/5	*v India, Lahore 1989/90*
West Indies	692/8d	*v England, The Oval 1995*
South Africa	682/6d	*v England, Lord's 2003*
India	676/7	*v Sri Lanka, Kanpur 1986/87*

Lowest Team Score

England	46	*v West Indies, Port of Spain 1993/94*
West Indies	47	*v England, Kingston 2003/04*
West Indies	51	*v Australia, Port of Spain 1998/99*
West Indies	53	*v Pakistan, Faisalabad 1986/87*
Pakistan	53	*v Australia, Sharjah 2002/03*
West Indies	54	*v England, Lord's 2000*
Pakistan	59	*v Australia, Sharjah 2002/03*
West Indies	61	*v England, Leeds 2000*
Pakistan	62	*v Australia, Perth 1981/82*
Zimbabwe	63	*v West Indies, Port of Spain 1999/00*

Ashes

Most Runs

SR Waugh	3,173
AR Border	3,076
DI Gower	2,617
MA Taylor	2,496
ME Waugh	2,204
GA Gooch	2,153
DC Boon	2,041
MA Atherton	1,900
AJ Stewart	1,810
MJ Slater	1,669

Most Wickets

SK Warne	132
GD McGrath	117
TM Alderman	100
GF Lawson	97
IT Botham	95
CJ McDermott	84
MG Hughes	75
D Gough	74
AR Caddick	64
JN Gillespie	62

Most Catches/Stumpings

IA Healy	135
AJ Stewart	84
AC Gilchrist	51
RW Marsh	51
AR Border	48
MA Taylor	46
ME Waugh	43
IT Botham	42
SR Waugh	29
RC Russell	28

Most Appearances

SR Waugh	45
AR Border	39
MA Atherton	33
IA Healy	33
AJ Stewart	33
MA Taylor	33
DI Gower	32
GA Gooch	31
DC Boon	30
ME Waugh	29

Best Ecomony Rates

RJ Bright	2.03
TBA May	2.13
JE Emburey	2.16
PH Edmonds	2.22
G Miller	2.32
EE Hemmings	2.33
SK Warne	2.34
PM Such	2.42
AD Mullally	2.46
BA Reid	2.53

Best Strike Rates

DW Headley	43.34
JR Thomson	44.07
GD McGrath	44.62
JN Gillespie	45.46
CJ McDermott	45.69
TM Alderman	47.17
BA Reid	48.36
PR Reiffel	50.56
D Gough	52.82
DK Lillee	53.39

Best Partnerships per Wicket

1st	GR Marsh & MA Taylor	329	
	Australia v England, Nottingham 1989		
2nd	DI Gower & GA Gooch	351	
	England v Australia, The Oval 1985		
3rd	DR Martyn & RT Ponting	242	
	Australia v England, Adelaide 2002/03		
4th	GP Thorpe & N Hussain	288	
	England v Australia, Birmingham 1997		
5th	AR Border & SR Waugh	332	
	Australia v England, Leeds 1993		
6th	DI Gower & CJ Richards	207	
	England v Australia, Perth 1986/87		
7th	MG Hughes & SR Waugh	147	
	Australia v England, Leeds 1989		
8th	GR Dilley & IT Botham	117	
	England v Australia, Leeds 1981		
9th	GF Lawson & SR Waugh	130	
	Australia v England, Lord's 1989		
10th	AJ Stewart & AR Caddick	103	
	England v Australia, Birmingham 2001		

Highest Individual Innings

JL Langer	250	*Australia v England, Melbourne 2002/03*
MA Taylor	219	*Australia v England, Nottingham 1989*
DI Gower	215	*England v Australia, Birmingham 1985*
N Hussain	207	*England v Australia, Birmingham 1997*
AR Border	200*	*Australia v England, Leeds 1993*
MTG Elliott	199	*Australia v England, Leeds 1997*
ML Hayden	197	*Australia v England, Brisbane 2002/03*
AR Border	196	*Australia v England, Lord's 1985*
GA Gooch	196	*England v Australia, The Oval 1985*
DM Jones	184*	*Australia v England, Sydney 1986/87*

Best Bowling

GD McGrath	8/38	*Australia v England, Lord's 1997*
RGD Willis	8/43	*England v Australia, Leeds 1981*
SK Warne	8/71	*Australia v England, Brisbane 1994/95*
CJ McDermott	8/97	*Australia v England, Perth 1990/91*
CJ McDermott	8/141	*Australia v England, Manchester 1985*
MS Kasprowicz	7/36	*Australia v England, The Oval 1997*
JN Gillespie	7/37	*Australia v England, Leeds 1997*
SCG MacGill	7/50	*Australia v England, Sydney 1998/99*
BA Reid	7/51	*Australia v England, Melbourne 1990/91*
PCR Tufnell	7/66	*England v Australia, The Oval 1997*

Highest Team Score

Australia	653/4d	*v England, Leeds 1993*
Australia	641/4d	*v England, The Oval 2001*
Australia	632/4d	*v England, Lord's 1993*
Australia	602/6d	*v England, Nottingham 1989*
Australia	601/7d	*v England, Leeds 1989*
England	595/5d	*v Australia, Birmingham 1985*
England	592/8d	*v Australia, Perth 1986/87*
Australia	576	*v England, Birmingham 2001*
Australia	552/9d	*v England, Adelaide 2002/03*
Australia	551/6d	*v England, Melbourne 2002/03*

Lowest Team Score

England	77	*v Australia, Lord's 1997*
England	79	*v Australia, Brisbane 2002/03*
England	92	*v Australia, Melbourne 1994/95*
Australia	104	*v England, The Oval 1997*
Australia	111	*v England, Leeds 1981*
England	112	*v Australia, Perth 1998/99*
England	114	*v Australia, Brisbane 1990/91*
Australia	116	*v England, Sydney 1994/95*
Australia	118	*v England, Birmingham 1997*
Australia	121	*v England, Birmingham 1981*

*Four Australia v England Tests in the time period where The Ashes were not at stake are not included in any stats for "The Ashes"
(2nd and 3rd Tests from the experimental 1979/80 series, the 1980 Centenary Test and the 1988 Bicentennial Test)*

Qualifications for Statistics:

	RO	Bowling Strike Rate	Batting Strike Rate
Tests	2000 balls	2000 balls	–
Ashes	1000 balls	1000 balls	–
ODIs	1000 balls	1000 balls	500 runs
World Cup	500 balls	500 balls	200 runs

One-day Internationals

Most Runs

SR Tendulkar	13,497
Inzamam-ul-Haq	10,267
SC Ganguly	9,914
ST Jayasuriya	9,896
M Azharuddin	9,378
PA de Silva	9,284
BC Lara	8,921
Saeed Anwar	8,823
ME Waugh	8,500
DL Haynes	8,202

Most Wickets

Wasim Akram	502
Waqar Younis	416
M Muralitharan	366
WPUJC Vaas	322
A Kumble	321
J Srinath	315
SM Pollock	305
SK Warne	291
GD McGrath	290
Saqlain Mushtaq	288

Most Catches/Stumpings

AC Gilchrist	326
Moin Khan	287
MV Boucher	265
IA Healy	233
Rashid Latif	220
RS Kaluwitharana	207
PJL Dujon	204
RD Jacobs	189
AJ Stewart	174
A Flower	173

Most Appearances

Wasim Akram	356
SR Tendulkar	342
M Azharuddin	334
ST Jayasuriya	328
Inzamam-ul-Haq	328
SR Waugh	325
PA de Silva	308
Salim Malik	283
A Ranatunga	269
SC Ganguly	266

Best Economy Rates

J Garner	3.04
RJ Hadlee	3.29
MA Holding	3.31
SP Davis	3.37
DK Lillee	3.40
AIC Dodemaide	3.40
AME Roberts	3.43
RGD Willis	3.48
CEL Ambrose	3.48
MD Marshall	3.53

Best Bowling Strike Rates

SE Bond	26.86
B Lee	28.60
AH Gray	28.86
GI Allott	29.38
Shoaib Akhtar	29.80
LS Pascoe	30.07
Saqlain Mushtaq	30.45
Waqar Younis	30.52
MS Kasprowicz	30.78
KSC de Silva	31.13

Best Batting Strike Rates

BL Cairns	105.59
AM Blignaut	105.54
Shahid Afridi	103.35
IDS Smith	99.43
RL Powell	98.20
Kapil Dev	95.27
AC Gilchrist	94.57
V Sehwag	94.05
A Flintoff	92.95
IVA Richards	90.69

Best Partnerships per Wicket

1st	SC Ganguly & SR Tendulkar	258
	India v Kenya, Paarl 2001/02	
2nd	R Dravid & SR Tendulkar	331
	India v New Zealand, Hyderabad (Decc) 1999/00	
3rd	R Dravid & SR Tendulkar	237
	India v Kenya, Bristol 1999	
4th	M Azharuddin & A Jadeja	275
	India v Zimbabwe, Cuttack 1997/98	
5th	A Jadeja & M Azharuddin	223
	India v Sri Lanka, Colombo (RPS) 1997	
6th	MO Odumbe & AV Vadher	161
	Kenya v Sri Lanka, Southampton 1999	
7th	HH Streak & A Flower	130
	Zimbabwe v England, Harare 2001/02	
8th	SK Warne & PR Reiffel	119
	Australia v South Africa, Port Elizabeth 1993/94	
9th	Kapil Dev & SMH Kirmani	126
	India v Zimbabwe, Tunbridge Wells 1983	
10th	IVA Richards & MA Holding	106
	West Indies v England, Manchester 1984	

Highest Individual Innings

Saeed Anwar	194	*Pakistan v India, Chennai 1997*
IVA Richards	189*	*West Indies v England, Manchester 1984*
ST Jayasuriya	189	*Sri Lanka v India, Sharjah 2000/01*
G Kirsten	188*	*South Africa v UAE, Rawalpindi 1995/96*
SR Tendulkar	186*	*India v New Zealand, Hyderabad (Decc) 1999/00*
SC Ganguly	183	*India v Sri Lanka, Taunton 1999*
IVA Richards	181	*West Indies v Sri Lanka, Karachi 1987/88*
Kapil Dev	175*	*India v Zimbabwe, Tunbridge Wells 1983*
ME Waugh	173	*Australia v West Indies, Melbourne 2000/01*
CB Wishart	172*	*Zimbabwe v Namibia, Harare 2002/03*
AC Gilchrist	172	*Australia v Zimbabwe, Hobart 2003/04*

Best Bowling

WPUJC Vaas	8/19	*Sri Lanka v Zimbabwe, Colombo (SSC) 2001/02*
GD McGrath	7/15	*Australia v Namibia, Potchefstroom 2002/03*
AJ Bichel	7/20	*Australia v England, Port Elizabeth 2002/03*
M Muralitharan	7/30	*Sri Lanka v India, Sharjah 2000/01*
Waqar Younis	7/36	*Pakistan v England, Leeds 2001*
Aaqib Javed	7/37	*Pakistan v India, Sharjah 1991/92*
WW Davis	7/51	*West Indies v Australia, Leeds 1983*
A Kumble	6/12	*India v West Indies, Kolkata 1993/94*
Imran Khan	6/14	*Pakistan v India, Sharjah 1984/85*
CEH Croft	6/15	*West Indies v England, Kingstown 1980/81*

Highest Team Score

Sri Lanka	398/5	*v Kenya, Kandy 1995/96*
India	376/2	*v New Zealand, Hyderabad (Decc) 1999/00*
India	373/6	*v Sri Lanka, Taunton 1999*
Pakistan	371/9	*v Sri Lanka, Nairobi (Gym) 1996/97*
South Africa	363/3	*v Zimbabwe, Bulawayo 2001/02*
England	363/7	*v Pakistan, Nottingham 1992*
West Indies	360/4	*v Sri Lanka, Karachi 1987/88*
Australia	359/2	*v India, Johannesburg 2002/03*
Australia	359/5	*v India, Sydney 2003/04*
South Africa	354/3	*v Kenya, Cape Town 2001/02*

Lowest Team Score

Zimbabwe	35	*v Sri Lanka, Harare 2004*
Canada	36	*v Sri Lanka, Paarl 2002/03*
Zimbabwe	38	*v Sri Lanka, Colombo (SSC) 2001/02*
Pakistan	43	*v West Indies, Cape Town 1992/93*
Namibia	45	*v Australia, Potchefstroom 2002/03*
India	54	*v Sri Lanka, Sharjah 2000/01*
West Indies	54	*v South Africa, Cape Town 2003/04*
Sri Lanka	55	*v West Indies, Sharjah 1986/87*
India	63	*v Australia, Sydney, 1980/81*
New Zealand	64	*v Pakistan, Sharjah, 1985/86*

World Cup

Most Runs

SR Tendulkar	1,732
PA de Silva	1,064
ME Waugh	1,004
RT Ponting	998
Javed Miandad	985
SR Waugh	978
A Ranatunga	969
BC Lara	956
Saeed Anwar	915
MD Crowe	880

Most Wickets

Wasim Akram	55
GD McGrath	45
J Srinath	44
AA Donald	38
WPUJC Vaas	36
CZ Harris	32
SK Warne	32
M Muralitharan	30
PAJ DeFreitas	29
A Kumble	28

Most Catches/Stumpings

AC Gilchrist	35
Moin Khan	30
AJ Stewart	23
MV Boucher	22
RD Jacobs	22
IA Healy	21
PJL Dujon	20
R Dravid	18
KS More	18
RT Ponting	18

Most Appearances

Wasim Akram	38
PA de Silva	35
J Srinath	34
SR Tendulkar	33
SR Waugh	33
Inzamam-ul-Haq	32
M Azharuddin	30
A Flower	30
A Ranatunga	30
Ijaz Ahmed	29

Best Economy Rates

CEL Ambrose	3.03
MD Marshall	3.08
CA Walsh	3.46
IT Botham	3.51
GR Larsen	3.52
AJ Traicos	3.57
SM Pollock	3.64
M Muralitharan	3.68
RA Harper	3.69
N Kapil Dev	3.70
GI Allott	3.70

Best Bowling Strike Rates

Waqar Younis	25.40
GI Allott	26.30
L Klusener	27.50
Imran Khan	27.54
Shoaib Akhtar	27.74
Saqlain Mushtaq	29.30
Z Khan	29.44
RMH Binny	30.00
ALF de Mel	30.11
SK Warne	30.53

Best Batting Strike Rates

L Klusener	121.17
JM Davison	118.94
N Kapil Dev	117.11
Moin Khan	106.31
SB Styris	101.90
Wasim Akram	100.70
RR Sarwan	95.87
AC Gilchrist	94.18
IVA Richards	92.89
AL Logie	91.85

Best Partnerships per Wicket

1st	Wajahatullah Wasti & Saeed Anwar	194
	Pakistan v New Zealand, Manchester 1999	
2nd	R Dravid & SC Ganguly	318
	India v Sri Lanka, Taunton 1999	
3rd	R Dravid & SR Tendulkar	237
	India v Kenya, Bristol 1999	
4th	LK Germon & CZ Harris	168
	New Zealand v Australia, Chennai 1995/96	
5th	CL Cairns & RG Twose	148
	New Zealand v Australia, Cardiff 1999	
6th	MO Odumbe & AV Vadher	161
	Kenya v Sri Lanka, Southampton 1999	
7th	RR Sarwan & RD Jacobs	98
	West Indies v New Zealand, Port Elizabeth 2002/03	
8th	DL Houghton & IP Butchart	117
	Zimbabwe v New Zealand, Hyderabad (Decc) 1987/88	
9th	N Kapil Dev & SMH Kirmani	126
	India v Zimbabwe, Tunbridge Wells 1983	
10th	J Garner & AME Roberts	71
	West Indies v India, Manchester 1983	

Highest Individual Innings

G Kirsten	188*	*South Africa v UAE, Rawalpindi 1995/96*
SC Ganguly	183	*India v Sri Lanka, Taunton 1999*
IVA Richards	181	*West Indies v Sri Lanka, Karachi 1987/88*
N Kapil Dev	175*	*India v Zimbabwe, Tunbridge Wells 1983*
CB Wishart	172*	*Zimbabwe v Namibia, Harare 2002/03*
AC Hudson	161	*South Africa v Netherlands, Rawalpindi 1995/96*
SR Tendulkar	152	*India v Namibia, Pietermaritzburg 2002/03*
PA de Silva	145	*Sri Lanka v Kenya, Kandy 1995/96*
R Dravid	145	*India v Sri Lanka, Taunton 1999*
A Symonds	143*	*Australia v Pakistan, Johannesburg 2002/03*
HH Gibbs	143	*South Africa v New Zealand, Johannesburg 2002/03*

Best Bowling

GD McGrath	7/15	*Australia v Namibia, Potchefstroom 2002/03*
AJ Bichel	7/20	*Australia v England, Port Elizabeth 2002/03*
WW Davis	7/51	*West Indies v Australia, Leeds 1983*
A Nehra	6/23	*India v England, Durban 2002/03*
SE Bond	6/23	*New Zealand v Australia, Port Elizabeth 2002/03*
WPUJC Vaas	6/25	*Sri Lanka v Bangladesh, Pietermaritzburg 2002/03*
KH MacLeay	6/39	*Australia v India, Nottingham 1983*
GD McGrath	5/14	*Australia v West Indies, Manchester 1999*
PA Strang	5/21	*Zimbabwe v Kenya, Patna 1995/96*
L Klusener	5/21	*South Africa v Kenya, Amstelveen 1999*

Highest Team Score

Sri Lanka	398/5	*v Kenya, Kandy 1995/96*
India	373/6	*v Sri Lanka, Taunton 1999*
West Indies	360/4	*v Sri Lanka, Karachi 1987/88*
Australia	359/2	*v India, Johannesburg 2002/03*
Zimbabwe	340/2	*v Namibia, Harare 2002/03*
Pakistan	338/5	*v Sri Lanka, Swansea 1983*
England	333/9	*v Sri Lanka, Taunton 1983*
India	329/2	*v Kenya, Bristol 1999*
South Africa	328/3	*v Netherlands, Rawalpindi 1995/96*
England	322/6	*v New Zealand, The Oval 1983*

Lowest Team Score

Canada	36	*v Sri Lanka, Paarl 2002/03*
Namibia	45	*v Australia, Potchefstroom 2002/03*
Scotland	68	*v West Indies, Leicester 1999*
Pakistan	74	*v England, Adelaide 1991/92*
Namibia	84	*v Pakistan, Kimberley 2002/03*
West Indies	93	*v Kenya, Poona 1995/96*
England	103	*v South Africa, The Oval 1999*
Kenya	104	*v West Indies, Kimberley 2002/03*
Bangladesh	108	*v South Africa, Bloemfontein 2002/03*
Sri Lanka	109	*v India, Johannesburg 2002/03*

World Cup Finals

Finals between 1980 and 2004

PRUDENTIAL WORLD CUP, 1983, FINAL

INDIA V WEST INDIES
Lord's, 25 June
India won by 43 runs
Toss: West Indies
Umpires: HD Bird and BJ Meyer
Man of the Match: M Amarnath

India innings

SM Gavaskar	c Dujon	b Roberts	2
K Srikkanth	lbw	b Marshall	38
M Amarnath		b Holding	26
Yashpal Sharma	c sub (AL Logie)	b Gomes	11
SM Patil	c Gomes	b Garner	27
*N Kapil Dev	c Holding	b Gomes	15
KBJ Azad	c Garner	b Roberts	0
RMH Binny	c Garner	b Roberts	2
S Madan Lal		b Marshall	17
+SMH Kirmani		b Holding	14
BS Sandhu	not out		11
Extras	(b **5**, lb **5**, w **9**, nb **1**)		20
Total	**(all out, 54.4 overs)**		**183**

FoW: **1**-2 (Gavaskar), **2**-59 (Srikkanth), **3**-90 (Amarnath), **4**-92 (Yashpal Sharma), **5**-110 (Kapil Dev), **6**-111 (Azad), **7**-130 (Binny), **8**-153 (Patil), **9**-161 (Madan Lal), **10**-183 (Kirmani)

Bowling	O	M	R	W
Roberts	10	3	32	3
Garner	12	4	24	1
Marshall	11	1	24	2
Holding	9.4	2	26	2
Gomes	11	1	49	2
Richards	1	0	8	0

West Indies

CG Greenidge		b Sandhu	1
DL Haynes	c Binny	b Madan Lal	13
IVA Richards	c Kapil Dev	b Madan Lal	33
*CH Lloyd	c Kapil Dev	b Binny	8
HA Gomes	c Gavaskar	b Madan Lal	5
SFAF Bacchus	c Kirmani	b Sandhu	8
+PJL Dujon		b Amarnath	25
MD Marshall	c Gavaskar	b Amarnath	18
AME Roberts	lbw	b Kapil Dev	4
J Garner	not out		5
MA Holding	lbw	b Amarnath	6
Extras	(lb **4**, w **10**)		14
Total	**(all out, 52 overs)**		**140**

FoW: **1**-5 (Greenidge), **2**-50 (Haynes), **3**-57 (Richards), **4**-66 (Gomes), **5**-66 (Lloyd), **6**-76 (Bacchus), **7**-119 (Dujon), **8**-124 (Marshall), **9**-126 (Roberts), **10**-140 (Holding)

Bowling	O	M	R	W
Kapil Dev	11	4	21	1
Sandhu	9	1	32	2
Madan Lal	12	2	31	3
Binny	10	1	23	1
Amarnath	7	0	12	3
Azad	3	0	7	0

RELIANCE WORLD CUP, 1987/88, FINAL

AUSTRALIA V ENGLAND
Eden Gardens, Calcutta
Australia won by 7 runs
Toss: Australia
Umpires: RB Gupta and Mahboob Shah (Pak)
Man of the Match: DC Boon

Australia

DC Boon	c Downton	b Hemmings	75
GR Marsh		b Foster	24
DM Jones	c Athey	b Hemmings	33
CJ McDermott		b Gooch	14
*AR Border	run out (Robinson/Downton)		31
MRJ Veletta	not out		45
SR Waugh	not out		5
Extras	(b **1**, lb **13**, w **5**, nb **7**)		26
Total	**(5 wickets, 50 overs)**		**253**

DNB: SP O'Donnell, +GC Dyer, TBA May, BA Reid

FoW: **1**-75 (Marsh), **2**-151 (Jones), **3**-166 (McDermott), **4**-168 (Boon), **5**-241 (Border)

Bowling	O	M	R	W
DeFreitas	6	1	34	0
Small	6	0	33	0
Foster	10	0	38	1
Hemmings	10	1	48	2
Emburey	10	0	44	0
Gooch	8	1	42	1

England

GA Gooch	lbw	b O'Donnell	35
RT Robinson	lbw	b McDermott	0
CWJ Athey	run out (Waugh/Reid)		58
*MW Gatting	c Dyer	b Border	41
AJ Lamb		b Waugh	45
+PR Downton	c O'Donnell	b Border	9
JE Emburey	run out (Boon/McDermott)		10
PAJ DeFreitas	c Reid	b Waugh	17
NA Foster	not out		7
GC Small	not out		3
Extras	(b **1**, lb **14**, w **2**, nb **4**)		21
Total	**(8 wickets, 50 overs)**		**246**

DNB: EE Hemmings

FoW: **1**-1 (Robinson), **2**-66 (Gooch), **3**-135 (Gatting), **4**-170 (Athey), **5**-188 (Downton), **6**-218 (Emburey), **7**-220 (Lamb), **8**-235 (DeFreitas)

Bowling	O	M	R	W
McDermott	10	1	51	1
Reid	10	0	43	0
Waugh	9	0	37	2
O'Donnell	10	1	35	1
May	4	0	27	0
Border	7	0	38	2

BENSON & HEDGES WORLD CUP, 1991/92, FINAL

ENGLAND V PAKISTAN
Melbourne (day/night), 25 March
Pakistan won by 22 runs
Toss: Pakistan
Umpires: BL Aldridge (NZ) and SA Bucknor (WI)
Man of the Match: Wasim Akram

Pakistan

Aamir Sohail	c Stewart	b Pringle	4
Rameez Raja	lbw	b Pringle	8
*Imran Khan	c Illingworth	b Botham	72
Javed Miandad	c Botham	b Illingworth	58
Inzamam-ul-Haq		b Pringle	42
Wasim Akram	run out		33
Salim Malik	not out		0
Extras	(lb **19**, w **6**, nb **7**)		32
Total	**(6 wickets, 50 overs)**		**249**

DNB: Ijaz Ahmed, +Moin Khan, Mushtaq Ahmed, Aqib Javed

FoW: **1**-20 (Aamir Sohail), **2**-24 (Rameez Raja), **3**-163 (Javed Miandad), **4**-197 (Imran Khan), **5**-249 (Inzamam-ul-Haq), **6**-249 (Wasim Akram)

Bowling	O	M	R	W
Pringle	10	2	22	3 (5nb 3w)
Lewis	10	2	52	0 (2nb 1w)
Botham	7	0	42	1
DeFreitas	10	1	42	0 (1w)
Illingworth	10	0	50	1
Reeve	3	0	22	0 (1w)

England

*GA Gooch	c Aqib Javed	b Mushtaq Ahmed	29
IT Botham	c Moin Khan	b Wasim Akram	0
+AJ Stewart	c Moin Khan	b Aqib Javed	7
GA Hick	lbw	b Mushtaq Ahmed	17
NH Fairbrother	c Moin Khan	b Aqib Javed	62
AJ Lamb		b Wasim Akram	31
CC Lewis		b Wasim Akram	0
DA Reeve	c Rameez Raja	b Mushtaq Ahmed	15
DR Pringle	not out		18
PAJ DeFreitas	run out		10
RK Illingworth	c Rameez Raja	b Imran Khan	14
Extras	(lb **5**, w **13**, nb **6**)		24
Total	**(all out, 49.2 overs)**		**227**

FoW: **1**-6 (Botham), **2**-21 (Stewart), **3**-59 (Hick), **4**-69 (Gooch), **5**-141 (Lamb), **6**-141 (Lewis), **7**-180 (Fairbrother), **8**-183 (Reeve), **9**-208 (DeFreitas), **10**-227 (Illingworth)

Bowling	O	M	R	W
Wasim Akram	10	0	49	3
Aqib Javed	10	2	27	2
Mushtaq Ahmed	10	1	41	3
Ijaz Ahmed	3	0	13	0
Imran Khan	6.2	0	43	1
Aamir Sohail	10	0	49	0

Wills World Cup, 1995/96, Final

AUSTRALIA V SRI LANKA
Lahore (day/night), 17 March
Sri Lanka won by 7 wickets
Toss: Sri Lanka
Umpires: SA Bucknor (WI) and DR Shepherd (Eng)
Man of the Match: PA de Silva

Australia

*MA Taylor	c Jayasuriya	b de Silva	74
ME Waugh	c Jayasuriya	b Vaas	12
RT Ponting		b de Silva	45
SR Waugh	c de Silva	b Dharmasena	13
SK Warne	st Kaluwitharana	b Muralitharan	2
SG Law	c de Silva	b Jayasuriya	22
MG Bevan	not out		36
+IA Healy		b de Silva	2
PR Reiffel	not out		13
Extras	(lb **10**, w **11**, nb **1**)		22
Total	**(7 wickets, 50 overs)**		**241**

DNB: DW Fleming, GD McGrath

FoW: **1**-36 (ME Waugh), **2**-137 (Taylor), **3**-152 (Ponting), **4**-156 (Warne), **5**-170 (SR Waugh), **6**-202 (Law), **7**-205 (Healy)

Bowling	O	M	R	W
Wickramasinghe	7	0	38	0
Vaas	6	1	30	1
Muralitharan	10	0	31	1
Dharmasena	10	0	47	1
Jayasuriya	8	0	43	1
de Silva	9	0	42	3

Sri Lanka

ST Jayasuriya	run out		9
+RS Kaluwitharana	c Bevan	b Fleming	6
AP Gurusinha		b Reiffel	65
PA de Silva	not out		107
*A Ranatunga	not out		47
Extras	(b **1**, lb **4**, w **5**, nb **1**)		11
Total	**(3 wickets, 46.2 overs)**		**245**

DNB: HP Tillakaratne, RS Mahanama, HDPK Dharmasena, WPUJC Vaas, GP Wickramasinghe, M Muralitharan

FoW: **1**-12 (Jayasuriya), **2**-23 (Kaluwitharana), **3**-148 (Gurusinha)

Bowling	O	M	R	W
McGrath	8.2	1	28	0
Fleming	6	0	43	1
Warne	10	0	58	0
Reiffel	10	0	49	1
ME Waugh	6	0	35	0
SR Waugh	3	0	15	0
Bevan	3	0	12	0

ICC World Cup, 1999, Final

AUSTRALIA V PAKISTAN
Lord's, 20 June
Australia won by 8 wickets
Toss: Pakistan
Umpires: SA Bucknor (WI) and DR Shepherd
Man of the Match: SK Warne

Pakistan

Saeed Anwar		b Fleming	15
Wajahatullah Wasti	c ME Waugh	b McGrath	1
Abdul Razzaq	c SR Waugh	b Moody	17
Ijaz Ahmed		b Warne	22
Inzamam-ul-Haq	c Gilchrist	b Reiffel	15
+Moin Khan	c Gilchrist	b Warne	6
Shahid Afridi	lbw	b Warne	13
Azhar Mahmood		c & b Moody	8
*Wasim Akram	c SR Waugh	b Warne	8
Saqlain Mushtaq	c Ponting	b McGrath	0
Shoaib Akhtar	not out		2
Extras	(lb **10**, w **13**, nb **2**)		25
Total	**(all out, 39 overs)**		**132**

FoW: **1**-21 (Wajahatullah), **2**-21 (Saeed Anwar), **3**-68 (Abdul Razzaq), **4**-77 (Ijaz Ahmed), **5**-91 (Moin Khan), **6**-104 (Inzamam-ul-Haq), **7**-113 (Shahid Afridi), **8**-129 (Azhar Mahmood), **9**-129 (Wasim Akram), **10**-132 (Saqlain Mushtaq)

Bowling	O	M	R	W
McGrath	9	3	13	2
Fleming	6	0	30	1
Reiffel	10	1	29	1
Moody	5	0	17	2
Warne	9	1	33	4

Australia

ME Waugh	not out		37
+AC Gilchrist	c Inzamam-ul-Haq	b Saqlain Mushtaq	54
RT Ponting	c Moin Khan	b Wasim Akram	24
DS Lehmann	not out		13
Extras	(lb **1**, w **1**, nb **3**)		5
Total	**(2 wickets, 20.1 overs)**		**133**

DNB: *SR Waugh, MG Bevan, TM Moody, SK Warne, PR Reiffel, DW Fleming, GD McGrath

FoW: **1**-75 (Gilchrist), **2**-112 (Ponting)

Bowling	O	M	R	W
Wasim Akram	8	1	41	1
Shoaib Akhtar	4	0	37	0
Abdul Razzaq	2	0	13	0
Azhar Mahmood	2	0	20	0
Saqlain Mushtaq	4.1	0	21	1

ICC World Cup, 2002/03, Final

AUSTRALIA V INDIA
Johannesburg, 23 March
Australia won by 125 runs
Toss: India
Umpires: SA Bucknor (WI) and DR Shepherd (Eng)
Man of the Match: RT Ponting

Australia

+AC Gilchrist	c Sehwag	b Harbhajan Singh	57
ML Hayden	c Dravid	b Harbhajan Singh	37
*RT Ponting	not out		140
DR Martyn	not out		88
Extras	(b **2**, lb **12**, w **16**, nb **7**)		37
Total	**(2 wickets, 50 overs)**		**359**

DNB: DS Lehmann, MG Bevan, A Symonds, GB Hogg, AJ Bichel, B Lee, GD McGrath

FoW: **1**-105 (Gilchrist), **2**-125 (Hayden)

Bowling	O	M	R	W
Khan	7	0	67	0
Srinath	10	0	87	0
Nehra	10	0	57	0
Harbhajan Singh	8	0	49	2
Sehwag	3	0	14	0
Tendulkar	3	0	20	0
Mongia	7	0	39	0
Yuvraj Singh	2	0	12	0

India

SR Tendulkar		c & b McGrath	4
V Sehwag	run out (Lehmann)		82
*SC Ganguly	c Lehmann	b Lee	24
M Kaif	c Gilchrist	b McGrath	0
+R Dravid		b Bichel	47
Yuvraj Singh	c Lee	b Hogg	24
D Mongia	c Martyn	b Symonds	12
Harbhajan Singh	c McGrath	b Symonds	7
Z Khan	c Lehmann	b McGrath	4
J Srinath		b Lee	1
A Nehra	not out		8
Extras	(b **4**, lb **4**, w **9**, nb **4**)		21
Total	**(all out, 39.2 overs, 180 mins)**		**234**

FoW: **1**-4 (Tendulkar), **2**-58 (Ganguly), **3**-59 (Kaif), **4**-147 (Sehwag), **5**-187 (Dravid), **6**-208 (Yuvraj Singh), **7**-209 (Mongia), **8**-223 (Harbhajan Singh), **9**-226 (Srinath), **10**-234 (Khan)

Bowling	O	M	R	W
McGrath	8.2	0	52	3
Lee	7	1	31	2
Hogg	10	0	61	1
Lehmann	2	0	18	0
Bichel	10	0	57	1
Symonds	2	0	7	2

Index

Picture Credits

Front Cover Philip Brown

Foreword & Introduction
2 Philip Brown; 5 Andy Clark/Reuters; 6 Patrick Eagar; 7 *top* Patrick Eagar; 7 *bottom* Matthew Impey;
8 Philip Brown; 9 Rebecca Naden/PA; 10 Laurence Griffiths/Getty Images; 11 David Davies/PA;
12 Mark Baker/Reuters; 13 Hamish Blair/Getty Images

The Domestic Game
14 Philip Brown; 15 Philip Brown; 16 Michael Steele/Getty Images; 17 Philip Brown;
18–19 Tom Shaw/Getty Images; 20 Adrian Murrell/Getty Images; 21 Chris McGrath/Getty Images;
22 *left* & *right* Philip Brown; 23 Adrian Murrell/Getty Images; 24 Patrick Eagar;
25 Scott Barbour/Getty Images; 26 Philip Brown; 27 *left* Robert Cianflone/Getty Images;
27 *right* Chris Turvey; 28 Darren Pateman; 29 Russell Cheyne/Getty Images;
30 Mark Thompson/Getty Images; 31 Patrick Eagar; 32 Shaun Botterill/Getty Images;
33 Tom Jenkins; 34 Jan Traylen; 35 Graham Morris; 36 Clive Mason/Getty Images;
37 Stu Forster/Getty Images; 38 Philip Brown; 39 Pete Norton; 40 Philip Brown;
41 Philip Brown; 42 Philip Brown; 43 David Gray/Reuters; 44 Mike Hutchings/Reuters;
45 Jonathan Wood/Getty Images; 46 Adrian Murrell/Getty Images; 47 *left* Ben Radford/
Getty Images; 47 *right* Adrian Murrell/Getty Images; 48 Graham Morris; 49 Philip Brown;
50 Philip Brown; 51 Graham Morris; 52 Patrick Eagar; 53 *top* Graham Morris;
53 *bottom* Scott Barbour/Getty Images; 54 Philip Brown; 55 Philip Brown;
56 Tom Shaw/Getty Images; 57 Philip Brown

The Tests
58 Philip Brown; 59 Patrick Eagar; 60 Patrick Eagar; 61 Hamish Blair/Getty Images;
62 Patrick Eagar; 63 Ben Radford/Getty Images; 64 Scott Barbour/Getty Images;
65 *top* Clive Mason/Getty Images; 65 *bottom* Hamish Blair/Getty Images; 66 Michael Steele/
Getty Images; 67 Laurence Griffiths/Getty Images; 68 *left* & *right* Philip Brown; 69 *left* Jack Atley;
69 *right* Tom Jenkins; 70 Clive Mason/Getty Images; 71 Adrian Murrell/Getty Images;
72 David Ashdown; 73 Philip Brown; 74 Philip Brown; 75 Nigel Marple/Reuters;
76 Hamish Blair/Getty Images; 77 Shaun Botterill/Getty Images; 78 Philip Brown;
79 Paul Gilham/Getty Images; 80 Patrick Eagar; 81 Rebecca Naden/PA; 82 *left* Graham Chadwick/Getty
Images; 82 *right* Philip Brown; 83 Chris Turvey; 84 Hamish Blair/Getty Images; 85 David Hancock
AFP/Getty Images; 86 Chris Cole/Getty Images; 87 *left* Philip Brown; 87 *right* Ben Radford/Getty
Images; 88 Ben Radford/Getty Images; 89 Mike Hewitt/Getty Images; 90 *left* Philip Brown; 90 *right*
Clive Mason/Getty Images; 91 *left* Hamish Blair/Getty Images; 91 *right* Paul Gilham/Getty Images; 92
Stu Forster/Getty Images; 93 Chris Turvey; 94–5 Rebecca Naden/PA; 96 Hamish Blair/Getty Images; 97
Stu Forster/Getty Images; 98 Tom Shaw/Getty Images; 99 Clive Rose/Getty Images; 100 Ben
Radford/Getty Images; 101 *left* & *right* Philip Brown; 102 Tom Shaw/Getty Images; 103 Tom
Shaw/Getty Images; 104–5 Patrick Eagar; 106 Patrick Eagar; 107 Hamish Blair/Getty Images; 108 *top*
Clive Mason/Getty Images; 108 *bottom* Adrian Murrell/Getty Images; 109 *top* & *bottom* Philip Brown;
110 Tom Jenkins; 111 Clive Mason/Getty Images; 112 Hamish Blair/Getty Images;
113 Clive Mason/Getty Images; 114 Philip Brown; 115 Scott Barbour/Getty Images;
116 Philip Brown; 117 Philip Brown

The Ashes
118 Adrian Murrell/Getty Images; 119 Steve Lindsell; 120 Adrian Murrell/Getty Images;
121 Adrian Murrell/Getty Images; 122 Philip Brown; 123 Patrick Eagar; 124 Laurence Griffiths/Getty
Images; 125 Patrick Eagar; 126 Patrick Eagar; 127 Patrick Eagar; 128 Patrick Eagar; 129 Michael
Regan/Action Images; 130 Graham Morris; 131 Philip Brown; 132 *top* Philip Brown;
132 *bottom* Patrick Eagar; 133 Philip Brown; 134 Philip Brown; 135 *left* Philip Brown;
135 *right* Graham Chadwick/Getty Images; 136–7 Jack Atley; 138 Philip Brown; 139 Jack Atley;
140 Patrick Eagar; 141 Philip Brown; 142 Philip Brown; 143 Patrick Eagar; 144 Ben Radford/
Getty Images; 145 *top* Patrick Eagar; 145 *bottom* Philip Brown; 146 Adrian Murrell/Getty Images;
147 Tom Jenkins; 148 Hamish Blair/Getty Images; 149 *left* Clive Mason/Getty Images;
149 *right* Tom Shaw/Getty Images; 150 Mike Hewitt/Getty Images; 151 Philip Brown;
152 Patrick Eagar; 153 *left* & *right* Philip Brown; 154 *top* Ben Radford/Getty Images;
154 *bottom* Philip Brown; 155 Patrick Eagar; 156–7 Patrick Eagar; 158 Philip Brown;
159 Patrick Eagar

The One-day Game
160 David Davies/PA; 161 Philip Brown; 162 Patrick Eagar; 163 Dave Cannon/Getty Images;
164 Philip Brown; 165 Hamish Blair/Getty Images; 166 Philip Brown; 167 Patrick Eagar;
168 Philip Brown; 169 *left* & *right* Philip Brown; 170 Clive Mason/Getty Images;
171 Clive Mason/Getty Images; 172 Philip Brown; 173 Philip Brown; 174 Tom Shaw/Getty Images;
175 Laurence Griffiths/Getty Images; 176 David Ashdown; 177 Russell Boyce/Reuters;
178 Patrick Eagar; 179 Ben Radford/Getty Images; 180 Tom Shaw/Getty Images; 181 Rob Elliott
AFP/Getty Images; 182 Jack Atley; 183 Scott Barbour/Getty Images; 184 Michael Regan/
Action Images; 185 David Gray/Reuters; 186 *left* & *right* Adrian Murrell/Getty Images;
187 *left* Philip Brown; 187 *right* Stu Forster/Getty Images; 188 Shaun Botterill/Getty Images;
189 Tom Shaw/Getty Images; 190 Clive Mason/Getty Images; 191 Patrick Eagar; 192 Clive Mason/Getty
Images; 193 Philip Brown; 194 Tom Shaw/Getty Images; 195 Hamish Blair/Getty Images;
196 ArkoDatta/Reuters; 197 Clive Mason/Getty Images; 198 Philip Brown; 199 Philip Brown;
200 Adrian Murrell/Getty Images; 201 Clive Rose/Getty Images

The World Cup
202 Mike Hutchings/Reuters; 203 Patrick Eagar; 204 Chris Cole/Getty Images; 205 Patrick Eagar;
206 Patrick Eagar; 206 *bottom* Shaun Botterill/Getty Images; 207 Ross Kinnaird/Getty Images;
208 Tom Jenkins; 209 Howard Burditt/Reuters; 210–11 Patrick Eagar; 212 *Top* David Davies/
Sportsphoto; 212 *bottom* Ross Kinnaird/Getty Images; 213 Patrick Eagar; 214 Clive Mason/
Getty Images; 215 Stu Forster/Getty Images; 216 Patrick Eagar; 217 Ben Radford/Getty Images;
218 Shaun Botterill/Getty Images; 219 *Top* Sucheta Das/Reuters; 219 *bottom* Howard Burditt/ Reuters;
220 Mike Hewitt/Getty Images; 221 Shaun Botterill/Getty Images; 222 *left* Philip Brown; 222 *right* Tom
Shaw/Getty Images; 223 David Gray/Reuters; 224 Philip Brown; 225 Patrick Eagar; 226 Philip Brown;
227 *top* Graham Morris; 227 *bottom* Joe Mann/Getty Images; 228 Mike Hewitt/Getty Images; 229
Patrick Eagar; 230 Adrian Murrell/Getty Images; 231 *top* Clive Mason/Getty Images; 231 *bottom* David
Gray/Reuters; 232 *top* & *bottom* Mike Hewitt/Getty Images; 233 Ross Kinnaird/Getty Images;
234 Andrew Cornaga/Photosport; 235 *top* & *bottom* Adrian Murrell/Getty Images; 236 Darren
Staples/Reuters; 237 Howard Burditt/Reuters

The Icons
238 Adrian Murrell/Getty Images; 239 Hamish Blair/Getty Images; 240 Tom Shaw/Getty Images;
241 Jack Atley; 242 Philip Brown; 243 *top* Ben Radford/Getty Images; 243 *bottom* Tom Shaw/
Getty Images; 244 Philip Brown; 245 Patrick Eagar; 246 Jack Atley; 247 *top* Philip Brown;
247 *bottom* Jon Buckle/Getty Images; 248 David Cannon/Getty Images; 249 Patrick Eagar;
250 Adrian Murrell/Getty Images; 251 Patrick Eagar; 252 Adrian Murrell/Getty Images;
253 *left* Patrick Eagar; 253 *right* Adrian Murrell/Getty Images; 254 Adrian Murrell/Getty Images;
255 Simon Bruty/Getty Images; 256 Darren England/Getty Images; 257 Graham Morris;
258 Shaun Botterill/Getty Images; 259 *left* Philip Brown; 259 *right* Reuters
260 Patrick Eagar; 261 Patrick Eagar; 262 Jack Atley; 263 Philip Brown; 264 *top* Philip Brown;
264 *bottom* Greg Wood/AFP/Getty Images; 265 Philip Brown; 266 ArkoDatta/Reuters;
267 Patrick Eagar; 268 Jewel Samad/AFP/Getty Images; 269 Matthew Impey; 270 Philip Brown;
271 Matthew Lewis/Getty Images; 272 *top* & *bottom* Graham Morris; 273 Philip Brown

The Future
274 Hamish Blair/Getty Images; 275 Mike Hewitt/Getty Images; 276 Hamish Blair/Getty Images;
277 Philip Brown; 278 *top* Philip Brown; 278 *bottom* Tom Shaw/Getty Images; 279 Hamish Blair/
Getty Images; 280 Graham Morris; 281 David Davies/PA; 282 Tom Shaw/Getty Images;
283 Jonathan Wood/Getty Images; 284 Graham Morris; 285 Clive Mason/Getty Images

Extras
286 Philip Brown; 287 Philip Brown; 288 *top* Ben Radford/Getty Images;
288 *bottom* Philip Brown; 289 Tom Shaw/Getty Images; 290 David Ashdown;
291 Patrick Eagar; 292 Philip Brown; 293 Philip Brown; 294 *top* Hamish Blair/Getty Images;
294 *bottom* Sarah Williams; 295 *top* & *bottom* Philip Brown; 296 *top* Graham Morris;
296 *bottom* Philip Brown; 297 Philip Brown; 298 Hamish Blair/Getty Images;
299 *top* Clive Mason/Getty Images; 299 *bottom* Arko Datta/Reuters; 300 *left* Simon Bruty/
Getty Images; 300 *right* Adrian Murrell/Getty Images; 301 *left* Hamish Blair/Getty Images;
301 *right* Matthew Lewis/Getty Images; 302 Graham Chadwick/Getty Images; 303 Philip Brown;
304 Michael Steele/Getty Images; 305 Jason O'Brien/Action Images; 312 Graham Morris

Back Cover Rebecca Naden/PA